FAR EAST
MEETS
FAR WEST

Searching for a Better Life
(A Personal Family Odyssey)

Evelyn

Evelyn Marvin Millman

E. Millman

 FriesenPress

Suite 300 - 990 Fort St
Victoria, BC, V8V 3K2
Canada

www.friesenpress.com

ISBN
978-1-4602-9751-3 (Hardcover)
978-1-4602-9752-0 (Paperback)
978-1-4602-9753-7 (eBook)

1. BIOGRAPHY & AUTOBIOGRAPHY, PERSONAL MEMOIRS

Distributed to the trade by The Ingram Book Company

To the memory of my parents, Jack and Betty Marvin, who gave my siblings and me life, love, and the spirits of endurance and enterprise.

Also dedicated to the memory of the following mentors
To Tom, my husband of 46 years and father of our three children, whose love, wise legal counsel, wit, integrity and honesty were second to none.

To my brother Jack, who always came back for every special occasion in my life.

To the Rev. George and Evelyn Edwards for their interest in our family and their gracious hospitality when I resided in their home for a short period.

To Dr. Ronald F. Watts for his patience and passion in guiding and teaching young people.

To Madame Phyllis Szeliga for taking me on as a favoured piano student when my finances were nonexistent.

To Gerhard Krapf, who admitted me to the Pipe Organ Performance program at the University of Alberta, for his passion in teaching church theology and liturgy as much as the pipe organ.

To my best friend Lis, whom I miss dearly.

And to Dr. Brian Evans, whose interest in all things Chinese and whose history classes and encouragement and support inspired me to write these family memoirs.

Table of Contents

CHAPTER ONE

A Personal Family Odyssey

"Each of us is the vehicle of the history which produced us."
—James Baldwin

The Mah Marvin Family

Our historical stories give us a feeling of belonging and self-esteem. When we know from whence we came, it helps us to know ourselves better and have pride in our beginnings.

A native minister speaking at a church service told a story of when he was a little boy and his grandfather took him and his father on a fishing trip. The grandfather knew of a secret place where the fishing was guaranteed. Only his grandfather knew of it. The boy was extremely excited because this was a new experience although he had fished with his father on the water's edge at home. His grandfather was his favourite person and highly respected by everyone.

They travelled to the spot, but before they could get to the water, they had to go through dense bushes. The grandson was a bit nervous because he didn't want to get lost there, but he was with his father and grandfather and knew they would keep him safe. They pushed the bushes aside and started to walk in. The little boy became quite frightened, but the grandfather told him it would be okay because he knew where he was going. They went a little farther, and the bushes became thicker, and it was getting darker inside the deep woods. The boy started to cry, so they all stopped for a moment, and the grandfather told his grandson a story.

"Look behind you and keep careful notice of what we have come through. When we come back, everything that was on our left side will be on our right side, and everything that was on our right side will be on our left side. On our pathway we must always keep careful watch on where and what we have come through in order to find our way back on the right path. There might be slight changes returning because we have bent the bushes to get through, but you will notice that most of what we have been through is still the same and will guide us on our homeward journey."

Telling the stories of our family's past is like that aboriginal story. There will be changes, but looking back into the past gives us a good sense of where (and who) we have come from. It will help to keep us on the right pathway in life, one that our forbearers worked so strenuously to provide.

Growing up we didn't think of asking very many questions of the family members that surrounded us—their beginnings or experiences—and unfortunately they didn't very often take the time to reveal much of their histories to us either. We would catch little snippets of stories from them from time to time, but when we were young these little bits of their personal lives left no impact on our developing minds. Perhaps they said little because they were so busy keeping body and soul together in a new and developing country that they didn't have the time or the inclination to do so. For them the present was all consuming. Our young nation and many of its peoples had not developed an oral tradition that existed in many older and more primitive cultures before print was developed. Then, storytelling was a way to keep the family history and culture alive. It was also a form of entertainment. Some members of a family were assigned the task of memorizing family stories that were then handed down through many future generations to memorize as well. It was important to be accurate and factual so only the best were chosen for this task.

In his book *Roots*, Arthur Haley writes that he physically journeyed back seven generations to the original village of his slave ancestor in present day Sierra Leone to make sure that the oral stories that were handed down to him through several ancestors by his mother and father were really true. To his utter surprise, after all the intervening years since his ancestor was captured by slave traders so many years ago, the current local unschooled storyteller in the old village told him the same stories via an interpreter. In the following pages are some of the stories I know and heard from various sources. These are the memories I have of my parents and our family that I have preserved in my mind.

I now wish I had known my parents better. This is another major reason why I feel compelled to write about them—so that our children will know what I didn't always know when I was growing up in our home. I know that the minutia of our lives will not be as important to others as it is to us, but our progeny deserve to know it, if not now, then perhaps later.

The following chapters are the story of my family as I try to walk in their shoes in a different era. In writing these memoirs, it is important to me to be as historically accurate as possible while at the same time filling in those intervals where no facts are possible—in other words, reading and writing between the lines. For this reason, the available historical documents and our family photos are the backbone for my memory around which I weave this story, except for what we, their children, lived and knew. Over the years, I have also gleaned some of this history from relatives and friends and their colleagues still living. I do not consider myself a storyteller in the sense that a tale can be embellished, embroidered and coloured to make it more exciting with facts that may or may not be true. I like to think of myself as more of a historian who tries to reveal how interesting and unique the actual truths and incidents in one's family's life are. However, to further round out what I have written, I have also included in the appendices some anecdotes, memories, and articles by members of my family

There were several roadblocks that interfered with our parents' ability to share their past with each other and with their children.

Interracial

Dad was Chinese from the southern part of China, and Mom was German from the Ukraine in Russia. In the thirties, this type of interracial marriage was extremely unusual and likely to raise a few eyebrows. These kinds of tensions were aptly portrayed in the movie *Guess Who's Coming to Dinner* and other movies of more recent times.

Intercultural

Dad was from the Far East while Mom was from the Far West. Their cultures were as different as black and white in many ways. They had different ways of raising children and different ideas of what girls and boys should do with their lives. In my brother Bill's writings, he states that his sisters were busy learning how to be ladies while he, and my brother Jack were doing the hard work on the farm. This was the prevailing attitude at that time, but it was also the difference between the two cultures. My sister and I never for one moment thought we were learning to be ladies because we did hard work too, in a different way, in the home as well as on the farm.

Age

Mom was twenty-two years Dad's junior. Dad was my grandmother's age so Mom and Dad really lived in different generational zones. However, Dad always had a youthful appearance and looked the same age as Mom for most of their lives. Mom told me later that she didn't know Dad's age when they got married. He looked so young. Somehow I doubt that age would have had any effect on her decision to marry him.

Language

Since neither knew the other's mother tongue, they had to communicate in English, which is not such a bad thing, but sometimes the thinking in one language can be different from another language and can lead to misunderstandings. However, I am sure they thought in English because, by the time they met, they had been thoroughly integrated into Canadian culture and its language even though they communicated with others in their mother tongues.

In Grande Prairie, Alberta, the simple gravestone below marks the final resting place of two remarkable and unique people: Mah Wing Chick, or Jack Marvin as he was known later, and Elizabeth Wiedeman or Betty Marvin after she got married.

In the Chinese language, the surname always comes first. Mah, which was my dad's Chinese surname, means *horse* in Chinese, thus you will notice from the photo that the symbol for horse is in the centre of the tombstone. Wing is sometimes the mother's birth surname and Chick the given name. The current Chinese character for horse appears below the horse and represents the evolution of several changes in its form since it was first used in the primitive Chinese glyphs. One could use their imagination to see how this character would represent the form of a horse as it finally evolved over several centuries.

GRAVESTONE OF PARENTS IN GRANDE PRAIRIE CEMETERY, ALBERTA

My mother's maiden name, Wiedeman, is German in its origin. From what we can ascertain, it stems from origins that have something to do with agriculture or manufacturing as they were known in the Germanic language before the Industrial Revolution, in much the same way that Millman might have been the original surname for a man who worked in a mill of some sort in the United Kingdom.

Our parents arrived here when Western Canada was still opening up. The threads of their lives reveal themselves so beautifully in our children and grandchildren who are all of different ethnic mixtures including that of their forefathers referred to in this memoir and in the following: English, Scottish, Palestinian, Vietnamese, Filipino, Swedish and Polish. Now we all enjoy the benefits of living in Canada because our parents lived frugally, worked hard, and overcame the original prejudices and problems of their initial immigrations. They made sure their children were inculcated with the morals and values important to them and encouraged them to get educations that made each one a useful citizen of our country.

CHAPTER TWO

Mah Wing Chick's Immigration

"Wherever you go, go with all your heart."
—Confucius

In 1903, Alberta was two years away from becoming a province in Canada. There were almost 78,000 people in Alberta at that time, and many of them would have been involved in agriculture, for there was very little infrastructure. Sir Wilfred Laurier was the Prime Minister of Canada, and Theodore Roosevelt was President in the United States. Henry Ford's Model T car wouldn't hit the assembly line for another five years (1908). The major mode of travel in all of Canada—besides boats and canoes on rivers, and walking—were the horse and buggy and the railway that had been completed in 1887. The thousands of Chinese workers that had been lured to Canada to work on the Canada Pacific Railway and had survived the appalling conditions to which they were subjected were immediately fired on the railway's completion and left to their own devices. Most immigrant Chinese men still wore their hair in pigtails or queues. The stories of what these Chinese men endured while employed during the building of the railway through the most treacherous parts of the mountains are horrendous to say the least. They had to bring their own tools and clothing. They made and ate their own food and were paid less than other immigrants who did the same jobs. The cloth shoes and cotton jackets that they wore in their homeland were certainly not adequate for the frigid temperatures they encountered during Canada's winters. Many of them perished on the mountain slopes and probably are still buried somewhere along the route. It is a national disgrace that still scars our Canadian conscience.

Mah Wing Chick did not immigrate to work on the railway; however, this is the Canadian world he found when he came here in 1903. British Columbia was already a province by the time he disembarked in Vancouver from the *Empress of India* at the age of fifteen, as the rather unofficially looking 1955 dated copy of his immigration letter confirms. He was described as a boy with no occupation from Hing Ying village in Sining, Southeast China, near the Pearl River. He was registered as C.I.5 #42334 and assigned File #873472. The Canada that he found upon his arrival was inhospitable and racist.

There was no welcoming committee or Social Service agency to help a young lad integrate into this land and no ESL (English as a Second Language) teachers, only federal immigration officers trying with great difficulty to translate the Chinese names into English. The prevailing culture in Canada was European. Most immigrants were English, German, Ukrainian, French, American, perhaps Scandinavian and Danish. Coming from a nation so different from Canada's basically European-flavoured environment must have been quite a culture shock for a young lad, but then young people adapt easily to changes.

Head Tax and Quarantine
Furthermore, upon his arrival in Canada, Mah Wing Chick suffered the same indignities as all the other young Chinese immigrants at that time. He was quarantined for a time to make sure he didn't bring in any diseases or infections and charged a head tax sum of $100. (This tax was later raised to $500). This was an especially huge sum of money in 1903 for entry into Canada. In today's terms it might have been equal to between $20,000 to $40,000 or even more. The great travesty of this head tax was that it was not applied to any of

C O P Y

CANADA

DEPARTMENT OF CITIZENSHIP AND IMMIGRATION
MINISTERE DE LA CITOYENNETE ET DE L'IMMIGRATION

IMMIGRATION BRANCH - DIVISION DE L'IMMIGRATION

OTTAWA, September 16th 1955.

TO WHOM IT MAY CONCERN:

Official Chinese Records show that one,
Mah Wing Chick, a native of Hing Ying, in the district
of Sinning, China, arrived at Vancouver, B.C. on September
16, 1903, ex the Empress of India and who at that time was
stated to be 15 years of age.

" L.W. Lloyd"
Chief, Immigration Records.

MAH WING CHICK'S 1903 CANADIAN IMMIGRATION PAPER

the other foreign immigrants. It was basically a way to limit entry of Chinese workers into Canada who were no longer needed to build the Canadian Pacific Railway.

How would Mah Chick have secured this amount of money? Would he have had to work in Canada for a long time to pay it off? Would he have secured it in China from somewhere or someone to whom he was beholden for a long time before it could be paid off? Or was it his family who borrowed the money, and would Mah Chick, as a loyal son, have sent money back to them to reimburse them for this loan as well as to support them financially? Was there an organization that made a lot of money off these initial immigrants? Was the organization illegal, requiring all the immigrants keep these details secret for fear that the authorities (Canadian or Chinese) might send them back to China? These are such interesting questions that linger in our minds so many years later. Maybe it is better for us not to know. Perhaps this is why our dad didn't seem to like talking about his early life in Canada. He might have wanted to forget those unhappy years of financial burden that were like a ball and chain to his freedom. Not only that, maybe he was afraid that his children might not be able to keep these secrets and, therefore, jeopardize his being in Canada.

Perhaps he discussed these issues with our mother, but if so, she didn't see it important enough to ever reveal to any of us. Maybe neither thought it necessary to relate anything about their past just as often happens to seniors nowadays about their early years. If nobody asks questions, who wants to know? So later in life, when one becomes more interested in preserving the experiences of our lives for the next generation, we glean what we can from reading about a nation's history, from asking questions of cousins and friends, from researching the limited documents and photos available to us in our own family files, from reading books about their times, and from researching what we can from the nation's archives and museums.

Christian Indoctrination at the Canton YMCA
It is rumoured that Mah Wing Chick came to Canada with an uncle, yet this fact cannot be verified by any of our Chinese family members.

We know that, in the Chinese culture, respectful young people often referred to their elders as aunt or uncle whether they were related to them or not. Perhaps Mah Chick was guided during his sea voyage and later in Canada by an older Chinese man who might have mentored Mah Chick on his entry. Before his voyage to Canada, it is known that Mah Chick stayed for a time at the YMCA in the Chinese city of Canton (now known as Guangzhou) before embarking on the ocean trip to Canada, Canton being a major ocean and shipping port in southern China at that time. This is probably where he received help in immigrating, where he received a Chinese bible and Christian indoctrination, where he received a Cantonese/English diction- ary and learned a bit of English, and where he was encouraged and supported in the challenges he was about to face in a new land. His indoctrination might have begun with English speaking missionar- ies in China who might have been active in the YMCA in Canton. Mah Chick's tattered dictionary resided in our home and eventually became my sister's possession. As a young child, I would often read it and try to say some of the words with the phonetics supplied to help one to pronounce the word or phrase. It didn't seem to help me much. My mother, who was zealous in her Christian outreach, gave Dad's Chinese Bible to one of the Chinese wives allowed into Canada later, after 1949, when the Government of Canada allowed the Chinese bachelors here to bring their families to Canada.

The YMCA (Young Men's Christian Association) was an organiza- tion that was born in London, England in 1844 by George Williams. The twenty-two-year-old Williams was moved to help young men who immigrated to that city and were in need of safe lodging, education and jobs. It was a charitable organization that quickly spread around the globe with an emphasis on Christian indoctrination through the help it offered to young men who were in great need in sometimes quite hostile environments.

Today the city of Canton (Guangzhou) is approximately a full day's journey, by car or bus, from Mah Chick's village situated in south China near the Pearl River delta. In the early 1900s, however, the automobile was not yet fully developed so we are not sure how he would have traversed the distance from his village to Canton other than by horse and buggy, rickshaw, bicycle or walking—in which case the journey would have taken *several* days. If his family lived near the river, he also could have taken a ferry, boat, or junk to Canton, stopping at various ports or towns along the way for these various transports to engage in shipping and trade.

Nowadays, when we contemplate a young lad of fifteen travelling on his own to a foreign country, we question the wisdom of parents allowing this. However, in the 1800s and early 1900s this was a common occurrence for young lads from many countries where poverty was common. The YMCA was created to help alleviate their immigration to new cities or countries although its present direction may have changed since then. It is difficult for our present family members to envision Dad with a pigtail or queue, but from historical records, he might have worn one when he came to Canada. The queue was prescribed for Chinese men by the Ching Dynasty from the seventeenth century onward as a symbol of their subjects' submission to the Ching dynasty and an indication of their loyalty to the ruling imperialists. It was abolished and banned in 1911 by the new Republic of China when the Ching dynasty was overthrown. Dad's earliest photo in our possession shows him with a western haircut that was taken five years after his arrival in Canada. Despite what I have just recounted here, it is also possible that the missionaries he encountered at the Canton YMCA five years earlier might have persuaded him to cut his queue off in favour of a western style so that he would fit better into the new land he would soon discover.

Influence of Dr. Sun Yat Sen and New Chinese Republic

Dr. Sun Yat Sen was the first president of the new Chinese republic and the founding father of modern China. He was almost regarded as a god by the Chinese in Canada and the United States. He had been educated in the West and wore his hair in a western-style cut when he visited many of the Chinese diasporic communities in Canada. He had been an example of how a Western-style haircut could help integrate the Chinese into their newfound communities and help reduce their curious image in this new country. When the queue was banned in China, it encouraged all of the Chinese bachelors in Canada also to cut their hair into a Western style.

The Rogers Sugar Shack?

My father was a great mystery to our family in many ways. He never talked of his early immigration days or his home and family in China. There are many questions around how he was able to come here, especially considering the sum of money he would have needed to pay for the head tax. Did he come with an uncle as was rumoured? What exactly happened to him when he landed in Vancouver other than what we know? Who did he work for? Did he get a wage, or was he beholden to someone for a period of time?

As I mention later in this book it seems entirely possible that he might have been employed by the Rogers family in Vancouver for a time. The Rogers family of sugar fame was renowned for employing Chinese immigrant lads in their home as cooks, gardeners and household servants. Our reasoning for this probability is that he later renewed a friendship with Philip Pon in Edmonton. Philip's adopted daughter mentions, in her memoirs, that her adopted dad was indeed one of the Rogers' employees when he first came to Canada before coming to Alberta. To our family, it seems clear that probably Philip Pon and Mah Chick had a previous relationship when they got together in the forties and fifties. We would not be privy to this since none of us understood the Chinese Cantonese dialect in which they conversed when they got together. At our young age, we would not have thought to ask either of them what they were talking about. Dr. Brian Evans, a Chinese scholar and professor of Chinese History at the University of Alberta, with his knowledge of the early Chinese in Canada, and especially in Alberta, feels that this was a very real possibility. Our family tends to accept his premise.

CHAPTER THREE

Gold Mountain:
First Years in Canada (1903)

Once the Chinese immigrants arrived...[in North America],
they found that the [so-called] gold mountain was an illu-
sion. Mining was uncertain work, and the gold fields were
littered with disappointed prospectors and hostile locals.
Work could be scarce, and new arrivals sometimes found it
difficult to earn enough to eat, let alone to strike it rich. Even
worse, they soon discovered that they were cut off from their
families: With no source of money, the immigrants could
not pay for their wives and children to make the long voyage
from China, and could not go back home themselves. As the
dream of gold faded, these men found themselves stranded
in a strange new land far from home. It was a land that did
not welcome them, a land that afforded them few means of
survival, and a land in which they were very much alone. —
Library of Congress website

[www.lcweb.loc.gov/teachers/classroommaterials/presentationsandactivities/pre-
sentations/immigration/chinese2.html]

Mah Chick's Family in China

Mah Chick was the second oldest in a family of either three or four brothers (this is unclear) and one older sister. He was chosen, like many other young Chinese men, to go to "Gold Mountain" to make a living and perhaps to become wealthy in order to support his parents and family back home. From our Chinese family sources in Canada, we surmise that Mah Chick's father, a man by the name of Mah Yee Lai, was considered fairly wealthy by the standards of his village at that time, for he had a factory where they dyed silk and cotton fabric. However, with the introduction of new technology in the fabric industry, his plant became outdated, and he was probably not able to finance new equipment in light of the disastrous economic situation all over China at that time. Mah Chick's father and uncle were teachers when the business was no longer important and were perhaps better educated than most. By all accounts, they were very good teachers. There was said to be about one hundred and fifty people in the village when Mah Chick left, so it was not large. Close by and across several rice fields was the Wong Village, and many of the young girls of Mah Chick's village were married to Wong bachelors and vice versa. This is most likely why so many Wongs and Mahs settled on the Canadian prairies in the early years of Chinese immigration. Immigrant family members kept in touch with their families back home in China and encouraged their migration to this new country to places where they already knew their kin here. Mah Chick's mother was named Mah Moi, and she was probably from the Wong village before their marriage.

The Gold Rush Frenzy

North America had earned the name "Gold Mountain" by the Chinese because they had heard rumours of the gold rushes in Canada and California. Thousands of young men, and not so young men, from all over the world rushed here in the 1800s hoping that their fortunes could be made quickly by joining the hordes who wanted to mine for gold in Canada and the United States. Most of the Chinese mined in the Caribou Mountains of British Columbia because they were not allowed to do so in the Yukon. Mah Chick did not come for the gold rush or for the railway work, however. The building of the Canadian Pacific Railway was finished by then, and the gold rush also was over in a few sad years, leaving many disillusioned, but still the excitement of the new country drew immigrants from all over the world.

Economic Disruption in China, Opium Wars
For ordinary citizens in China during the nineteenth and early twentieth centuries, the Opium Wars and the Taiping Rebellion had created a time of extreme economic disruption, a time of political uncertainty and change, and a time of growing discontent with the foreign powers that were very influential there. Although it is understood that Mah Wing Chick's father owned a simple fabric-dying operation in his village, this was becoming an obsolete industry with more modern technologies emerging. Even though his father and uncle were teachers, the disastrous economic situation all over China hit all families hard, so it might have seemed reasonable to groom Mah Chick for a new adventure in Canada for the family's sake in China. Who knows, maybe he wanted to leave and escape the poverty and political uncertainty. He was like his own sons later, spontaneous, difficult to hold down, and full of vim, vigour and adventure. However, his parents could hardly have understood the problems that their young son would face in Canada.

Working Eastward Through the Kootenay Rockies
Mah Chick worked as a houseboy in Vancouver for some time until he felt comfortable with the Canadian culture and language and—if we read between the lines again—to pay off his debts. Many young Chinese lads worked as houseboys for wealthy families in British Columbia for a period of time in homes like the Rogers Mansion (known as the Sugar Shack) where they learned how to cook Western-style food, do gardening chores, deliveries and house cleaning while at the same time learning the English language.

MAH CHICK'S 1908 PHOTO TAKEN IN VANCOUVER

After this stint in Vancouver, he made his way slowly across the western provinces, via such places as Nelson and Trail in British Columbia, working in restaurants along the way for short periods until he landed in Winnipeg. He had heard that there was not as much racism against the Chinese in Manitoba as there was in British Columbia, so he set his sights towards that city by working his way along the southern areas of the western provinces. It is quite possible that he also stopped along the way in Calgary since he seemed to know his way around there quite well. In our early years, Dad took us to visit the goldfish ponds and gardens of a brewery near the Bow River in the middle of the city. Did he spend a short time there working at odd jobs in that area? The brewery still exists today, but the pools have disappeared, and the gardens have been radically reduced from the beauty they once displayed in years gone by.

CHAPTER FOUR

Mah Wing Chick's Wider Chinese Family

We do not know a lot about Mah Chick's Chinese family except that his sister married a Wong from a nearby village in China and immigrated to Canada with her husband before Chinese wives and families were excluded from entering Canada with the Chinese Exclusion Act of 1923. Canada was willing to use cheap Chinese labor to help build the Canadian Pacific Railway, but other than that our nation was not interested in allowing Chinese immigration of their families. There was a kind of fear of the unknown that Canada would suddenly be flooded with Chinese immigrants. Is it possible that Mah Chick might have helped provide the funds for his sister's and her husband's immigrations? Like all the other mysteries, we do not know this, but it has always been common practice to help fund the immigration of one's relatives to a given area in a kind of chain reaction of migration.

Mah Gim Thiel and Wong Chung Ark

Mah Gim Thiel and Wong Chung Ark became Auntie and Uncle to us. They resided in Kelowna where they had a laundry business like many of the early Chinese who immigrated to Canada at the beginning of the 1900s. Their Hop Lee Laundry was also where they lived with their family close to the centre of the city near the hotels, which were

MAH CHICK WITH SISTER AND HUSBAND C. 1942

their best customers. Their unpainted shop contained all the early laundry equipment of that day—galvanized and wooden washtubs and hand irons that had to be heated on the stove. There was little electrical equipment and, because their major customers were the hotels, all laundry had to be neatly ironed. This was particularly exhausting in the hot summer days that were the norm in the Okanagan Valley. Air conditioning was unknown at that time.

Except for the Chinese community, Uncle never really integrated into the larger Kelowna community because he was always so busy with his laundry business, and furthermore, his grasp of English was quite limited. He always looked exhausted and thin. He was not an educated man, and even after many years in Canada, he seemed resistant to any changes from what he knew from his youth—in other words, very old fashioned compared to Mah Chick. When we visited them, their conversations were entirely in Cantonese, for Auntie had not learned English, a fact that completely isolated her for her entire life.

Uncle's Other Wife in China

Uncle had a second wife in China who never immigrated, and it must have kept him busy trying to support everyone. At that time, there was a tradition among the Chinese that it was important to have a part of you left in China whether it be land or a wife or a family so that, when you died, your body could be buried back in the homeland. This is a tradition that still seems to exist today in many families of different cultures. Canada was not your final resting place or home. It was just a stopping off place in your life journey where you could make a living, but when you grew older and could no longer work, you could go back to your homeland and be wealthy and be cared for. It seems that Uncle must have married this second wife on one of his visits back to China because he had one son, Tony, who was much younger than the children from Mah Gim Thiel.

Tony later immigrated to Kelowna where he eventually opened a Chinese restaurant. Unlike his father, Tony and his wife were friendly and welcoming, a good quality for a restauranteur. He and his family were included in one of our Mah family reunions. We often visited his restaurant when travelling through Kelowna and were always cordially welcomed.

Again, we are left with some nagging questions. Did our father have something to do with bringing his sister and husband to Canada? Did he want his sister to have the better life that he was beginning to enjoy?

Foot Binding of Young Girls

Auntie was always so glad to see Dad when we visited. It was probably one of the few times she was able to communicate with anyone from her immediate family. She didn't seem like a very happy woman except when she saw her brother. Fate had dealt her a very cruel blow during her lifetime. She had suffered through the agonizing foot binding in her early childhood and hobbled around their home in cloth shoes. Foot binding was a very common practice for young girls in China until it was abandoned in the later part of the nineteenth and early twentieth centuries. It was usually perpetrated on the firstborn girl from a wealthy family during their early years between four and seven so that she would be more attractive to a future husband. It was meant to keep her feet small and dainty, but most of the time it caused severe deforming of the feet and a great deal of excruciating pain for the victim. In most cases the toes had to be broken so they could be turned under and then bound. This cruel, barbaric practice was deemed to be erotically and sexually pleasing for the men. We wonder what kind of men would allow such a thing to happen to small children. In our twentieth century enlightenment, it seems akin to childhood sexual abuse of young girls and boys. Now that I understand a lot more about this abandoned and cruel system for Chinese girls, I would have made more of an effort to communicate with this auntie of mine when we visited. As my mother demonstrated so many times in her life with Dad, communication is possible even when one doesn't understand each other's language.

Summer Visits

We visited Dad's sister several times during our school summer holidays. The first time, in 1942, we travelled by train through the mountains completely entranced by the huge mountains in the Banff, Lake Louise, and Field areas. It was the first time we had seen such mountains and as we viewed these immense structures from the windows of our speeding train we were speechless, which must have been nice for our parents. We spent most of our time looking out the open train windows. The trains in those days were powered by coal and steam, so the soot and smoke came into our cabins leaving me with headaches and nausea. Several times the boys lost their caps to the wind as they stuck their heads out the windows. At the time, the steam locomotive, the beautiful mountains, and the open windows were a great attraction and adventure for us kids, but when we contemplate it now, with our twenty-first century safety sensibilities, it was a most dangerous thing to do. On that first trip, we boarded the train in Grande Prairie on the old Northern Alberta Rail line to Edmonton and then transferred somewhere along the line to another train that took us to Kelowna.

MAH GIM THIEL'S KELOWNA FAMILY MEMBERS

Uncle had six children with Auntie, three of whom lived in Canada during their youth. We got to know two of them quite well.

The third one lived in Unity, Saskatchewan, with her husband, James Mar, and they had a restaurant called The Paris Café. They had six children (Anita, Mae, Lily, Tom, Dean, and Jean) with whom we were not in contact until later when most of these cousins moved to Edmonton. We got to know these kin quite well, attending their weddings and Chinese dinners and other social events through the years.

The other three older children lived mostly in Hong Kong, and we did not get to know them at all. However, on one of our China tours, we did look up one of these cousins who had a model airplane shop in the downtown, but we were not there long enough to establish a relationship.

After Auntie's husband died, her children arranged for her to spend the rest of her life in a seniors' home where she lived in a fair amount of isolation because of her inability to converse in English. To me, it was one of life's great tragedies.

THE JIM MAR SASKATCHEWAN FAMILY C. 1990

Wong Syen Law, or Sunny

Auntie's daughter, Wong Syen Law—or Sunny as we called her—became a nurse and eventually married a Chinese doctor in Minneapolis. They had four sons. Two became medical doctors, one became a dentist and one became a lawyer. Denis, the lawyer, spent considerable time in Beijing learning mandarin and teaching at the University of Beijing there. He now resides in Seattle with the rest of his brothers and aging parents.

SUNNY'S FAMILY

Wong Suey Lee

Auntie's son, Wong Suey Lee, was not happy in Kelowna with the racism he experienced there. His father was very strict, old fashioned, and at times angry with Suey for working at better paying jobs in the Okanagan orchards and fruit wholesalers while he attended high school instead of in the family laundry. As one might expect, there was considerable tension in the family because Uncle needed to send money to China to support his wife and family there, leaving little for his Canadian family and wife here. Suey, being more Canadian than Chinese, eventually went to the United States and became an American citizen once he graduated from high school. He joined the US army and fought in the Korean War for the Americans.

SUEY IN US MILITARY UNIFORM

While overseas he was severely wounded, recuperating for a year in a Japanese hospital and was finally decorated by the US army. With financial assistance as an army veteran, he got his electrical engineering degree on his return to the United States and ran a successful consulting electronic engineering firm in California called Components Technology West which specialized in HiRel semiconductor devices and magnetic components.

Our family always kept in touch with these two cousins, especially Suey, visiting them in their various locations and inviting them to Edmonton whenever we had a Mah family reunion.

On his retirement, Suey settled in Green Valley, Arizona, south of Tucson where he died alone of Parkinson's Disease in December of 2013. His Parkinson's affliction might have been a result of the post-traumatic stress that was left undiagnosed from the Korean War and an earlier heart attack that also was a result of PTSD that a

SUEY AND WIFE EVA

THE WIDER MAH FAMILY REUNION C. 1990

Far East Meets Far West

veteran's doctor did diagnose later in his life. Eva, Suey's wife, was a Brazilian nurse, whom he adored, but she predeceased him by several years, falling victim to cancer. He and Eva had no children, but his family became the many Korean veterans who helped him greatly during his final illnesses.

Willie Wong

In Kelowna we also got to know another Chinese fellow. Willie Wong was a friend of Suey's and worked in one of the local hotels on Kelowna's main street. Willie's wife was still in China, but he took a liking to all of us children, and we remained friends throughout his life. His friendliness to our family made us feel as though he belonged to us. Eventually he was able to bring his wife and son, Richard, to Canada where they finally settled in Calmar, Alberta, and opened a small restaurant there. When they eventually retired to Edmonton, our mother befriended Willie's wife even though Mom could not speak Chinese, and Willie's wife could not speak English. Again this was one of the traits that set Mom apart from other Caucasian ladies who married Chinese men. She patiently made an attempt to communicate and be friendly to these women when they finally arrived in Canada to join their husbands. The Chinese women loved her even though they could not communicate in each other's language. After his education, Richard came to Edmonton to go to university and then got a job as a salesman in a local car dealership. He, too, was always included in our family reunions.

We do not know much about the other members of Dad's family in China except that Mah Biel, his younger brother, became addicted to opium—a great tragedy for his family during the years when the British were pushing East Indian opium contraband to the Chinese in exchange for buying their Chinese goods. The famous but disgraceful Opium Wars were partly an attempt by the British to open China to more trade and more ports, but the Chinese wanted to restrict their influence and the importation of opium that was destroying their economy and their people. The British were at the downhill peak of their international colonization mode during this historical period when they did basically win the wars. The Chinese, however, were on the uphill battle of ridding their country of their imperialist rulers as well as the foreign powers.

In 1986 when our family visited Dad's village, there were still a very few distant family members there, mostly elderly women; however, most had moved on to Hong Kong when the communists took over China and are not well known to us. I will touch on the emotional journey to visit Dad's village later.

CHAPTER FIVE

Winnipeg Period (1909-28)

New Destination

We know Mah Chick worked in Trail and Nelson, British Columbia, because many years later, after one of our visits to see Auntie in Kelowna, we travelled by car to Osoyoos, turning east up the steep switchback hairpin turns of the west side of the Cascade Mountains. In the back seat, we children did our best to help Dad drive the car, or so we thought, because we were afraid we might plunge over the side of these treacherous, narrow roads at any moment. Towards the summit, the clouds settled down upon us. We had to travel very slowly and eventually stop. We pulled off to a slight widening in the road where Dad gave Mom a big hug to reassure her that we could now relax because we had traversed the worst part of the road. Although Dad did not indicate it, I think he was as frightened as the rest of us. But at this point all I wanted to do was get out of the car and expel all the contents of my stomach somewhere. This childhood motion sickness plagued me for most of my life until I married Tom, a naval officer, and went to sea with him, finally curing myself of most of it. However, in my youth, my dad had little patience with these frequent episodes, and most of the time I just had to hang my head out of the car window and do my thing. When we finally landed in both Trail and Nelson—and other towns along the way—Dad took time to visit all his old restaurant haunts while the rest of us explored the various places in the towns and waited for him to finish his rendezvous with former Chinese friends.

We have no records or information about Dad working his way towards Winnipeg in parts of Alberta and Saskatchewan, but it seems that Winnipeg was where he was headed when he left Trail and Nelson in southern British Columbia. We feel he might have also stayed or toured the city of Calgary because, as children, we spent considerable time at the Molson Brewery gardens and fish ponds on our way to Kelowna in the forties. Dad seemed to know his way around there quite well and spent considerable time inspecting the garden and fish pond site. The brewery was known to employ immigrants in its workforce, so it begs the question: Did Mah Chick find temporary work there in the gardens while en route to Winnipeg? Was he interested in seeing what had been accomplished there in the interim?

Today the gardens and fish ponds are gone and the brewery is being considered for a heritage site as its buildings and site are one of the oldest in Calgary dating back to the late 1800s. However, in the forties, it was a fun place for children to explore with its goldfish, bridges and streams, and beautiful gardens.

In the early twentieth century, Winnipeg was recognized as the cultural capital of Western Canada. There seemed to be less racism there than in Vancouver, Victoria, and other British Columbia towns. When Mah Chick finally reached Winnipeg, sometime around 1907 or 1908 after his various jobs along the way, he apparently stayed at the YMCA there, joining the many other young men from various parts of the world, most notably those of Irish descent who were escaping the great potato famine in Ireland. This period seemed to have been a very happy time for him because he not only worked hard in the restaurants there as a cook but managed to improve his English and make friends with the rest of the Chinese bachelors there, as well as other Caucasians. He was gradually becoming Canadianized so to speak.

Chinese Christian Association/Winnipeg

Like other Chinese men, Mah Chick joined the Chinese Christian Association in Winnipeg which consisted of fifty-two other Chinese

緬省 華人基督教

Der Yoen Seu
Joe We
Wong Chee
Woo King Sue
Gin Wai
Gin Wing Erd
Yee Shang
Jim Mar King
Joe Kim
D. San Lee
Ma Seung
S. T. Pong
Fong Loo
Gin Pong Chow
Lee Key
Peter Mar
S. F. Ricketts
Gin Wing Dip
Fong Goong
Wong Ming
Wong Ki
Jim G. Williams
P. F. B
Wong Lim Nam
Gin Kim
J. W. Williams
W. K. Qung

1918 CHINESE CHRIS
WINN

Evelyn Marvin Millman

CHINESE CHRISTIAN ASSOCIATION

Far East Meets Far West

THE DEPARTMENT OF THE INTERIOR.

CHINESE IMMIGRATION BRANCH.

C. I.
9

No. 23920

JAN 3 - 1914, *19th* 1914

To the Collector of Customs,

Port of Vancouver

I hereby give notice that I desire to leave Canada with the intention of returning thereto. I propose to sail or depart from Vancouver for Hong Kong.

on the Empress of Asia day of JAN 3 - 1914 191

I intend to return to Canada at the port of (1) Vancouver

I request registration and I attach my photograph hereto and give the following information for the purpose of my identification on my return.

My proper name is *Mah Wing Chick*

I am sometimes known as *W. W. Jackson*

I first came to Canada in the year *1903 (Vancouver Empress India)*

My place of residence in Canada is *Winnipeg*

Where I have resided since the year *7 years*

Certificate of Registration Form C. I. 5 No. *Substitution applied for*

My present occupation is that of *Cook*

My place of birth was *Hing Ying*

My present age is *25*

Height *5* feet *4½* inches.

Facial marks or other peculiarities :—
Pit between eyebrows
" *right temple*
scar each eyebrow

I am personally known to *Mah Huey* and *Mah Kee* both of *Vancouver* to whom I would refer you for correctness of statements herein made.

馬榮植

(Signature of Chinese Person.)

I have personally examined the person of Chinese origin who claims to be the person above the photograph attached hereon (2), who returned to Canada on the , and declare him to be the same person.

(Controller.)

191

(Side text, right margin:) Particulars and photograph hereon shown compared with statement and approved by me this day. Dated at Vancouver JAN 3 - 1914 , 191

(Side text:) Released Victoria S. S. Tacoma Maru

[OVER.]

馬來永出口之身只經發還 所用以憑驗對 船是船的於 四月 日由本埠開行者

IMMIGRATION DOCUMENT 1914

Evelyn Marvin Millman

men. This group was organized and guided by clergymen from the Presbyterian and Methodist Churches. We feel this group had a strong connection to the YMCA although the 1918 photo does not indicate this. By now Mah Chick would have been twenty-eight years old and might have been in Winnipeg for several years.

In Winnipeg there were several important influences on Mah Chick's life, the YMCA perhaps being the most important because of the brotherhood of many young Chinese men and the Christian influence of its leaders. We can also imagine the singsongs around the piano with the Irish boys at the Y and the camaraderie that results when new immigrants get together to learn English and to venture into a new and different world. It soon became apparent that the young Mah Chick had some special talents—he had an exceptionally good baritone voice and wasn't afraid to use it in the sing-alongs. He was still fairly young, energetic, adventurous and anxious to make it in this new environment. He must have used his spare earnings to enlist in elocution and vocal classes where he learned to speak perfect English as well as to sing it. On many occasions, with the influence of his vocal teacher, he was invited to sing in some of the Winnipeg churches. He acquired a large collection of the popular music of the day as well as church music, which I still have in my possession to this day.

In many ways, this Winnipeg period for the Chinese bachelors was a better time for immigrant Chinese men than in other areas in Canada and in other nations, I presume. The Chinese Christian Men's Association gave the lonely men a chance to get to know each other and to communicate with Caucasian Canadians who could help them integrate and become more familiar with Canadian society. Like our current nation's response to the various refugee programs towards the Vietnamese, the Somalis, the Ugandans, the Ethiopians, the Syrians and many others, there seemed to be a caring concern for the Chinese at that time that perhaps did not exist for those poor souls who worked on the railroad.

A Shocker About the Past

An extremely interesting event happened in 1914, one that needs to
be touched on here in the middle of Mah Chick's Winnipeg sojourn
and which we did not know about until 1986 when my siblings and
I arranged a tour of China with our spouses. We solicited help from
our cousin Sam Mah in Grande Prairie to give us some information
about what we might expect should we arrange to visit Dad's village
while we were there. I shall elaborate on this visit later in this project
in order not to digress too much right now. Sam is a distant cousin
who arrived in Grande Prairie in 1949 and who lived in Mah Chick's
village before he left for Canada. However, here is the shocker for all
of us. Sam asked us whether we wanted to also visit the family of the
girl that Dad had married in China.

"What are you talking about?" we asked.

It soon became obvious that there were some things we did not
know about our dad, and Sam was not aware that we weren't clued
in. With all of our Christian sensibilities, to say that we were shocked
to hear this would be an extreme understatement. None of us knew.
Did our mom know it when she married Dad? We had to get over
this news before we made any further plans, but we had to keep our
mouths shut for Mom's sake in case she was not aware. If she did not
know, we did not want to alarm her at this stage in her life. Dad had
died in 1964, so we couldn't discuss it with him. We shouldn't have
been so shocked because we already knew of other Chinese men who
had two wives—one in China and one in Canada—including our Uncle
Wong in Kelowna. Now we are all aware that, at that time, we had a
certain image of our dad while growing up that Dad didn't want to
destroy by revealing all his secrets.

On February 24, 1914, Mah Chick was registered as C.I.28 #5411,
age 25. His address was listed as Winnipeg and documents stated
that he was also known as M.W. Jackson prior to embarking on his
ocean journey.

Dad returned to China on January 3, 1914, aboard the *Empress of
Asia* bound for Hong Kong and did not return until December 2, 1914,
aboard the *Tacoma Maru*. He was obviously going home to China for

the first time since his arrival in Canada. And he was probably going home to get married to a girl his parents had picked out for him— as was still the custom for Chinese families. Over the years we have become accustomed to the importance for Chinese young people to be married at certain ages. Most of these marriages are usually arranged by the parents. Mah Chick's mother would have been very insistent about this matter, and Mah Chick was, therefore, fulfilling his duty as a son. My mother often said to me that Dad had always been very fond of his mother and certainly would not have wanted to offend her or the Chinese customs about marriage.

Special Antique Trunk

Another interesting fact about this journey is that Mah Chick had a very special trunk built for him by a Winnipeg firm for his journey back to his Chinese family home. In 2014, this trunk was 100 years old and has become a valuable antique in our home. This strong well-built trunk is fashioned of thick reddish brown leather and brass fixtures and is much larger than most trunks of our day. It definitely would have been built to withstand the long arduous ocean voyages in the ships of 1914. It has Mah Chick's initials painted in silver grey on the outside of it: MWJ. Probably it was packed not only with Mah Chick's travelling clothes but with gifts and other things that he knew would meet the approval of his family members and his bride. On his return, he might have brought embroidered silk pictures to decorate his apartment and other things that adorned our home while we grew up.

Except for what Sam Mah has told us here, we will elaborate about this journey and what happened in China later. So let's return to Winnipeg where Mah Chick returned after almost a year in China. It seems that Mah Chick had become thoroughly Canadian and that, after almost eleven years in Canada, he could no longer feel comfortable in his family's home in China. In much the same way that he endured culture shock on entering Canada as a new immigrant, he would also have felt the opposite culture shock of returning back to the home and country of his youth. We can surmise that his recent marriage to the Chinese girl his parents had chosen for him was not fulfilling his desire for love nor did it look like it would produce any children. There was no compelling reason for him to remain in China and no hope that his new wife could immigrate to Canada. His immigration document indicated that he wished to return to Canada, and that is exactly what he did.

ANTIQUE TRUNK

A New Name and Singing Career

On his return, and with encouragement from his mentors, Mah Chick dared to think that he might venture into the world of vaudeville, which today we might call light opera or operetta or musicals. In order to do this, he knew that a Chinese name would never make it at that time in our Canadian history. Earlier he had made plans to anglicize his name, fearing that a Chinese sounding name might be a hindrance to his hoped-for career choice. In the 1918-1919 Chinese Christian Association photo his photo shows his new name as Jack Marvin in the bottom second row 4th from the right. Obviously he had toyed with the idea of a name change since the 1914 immigration document indicates that he was also known as M.W. Jackson. He finally did the unthinkable and legally changed his Chinese name from Mah Wing Chick to Jack Marvin. Mah Wing became Marvin and Chick became Jack. Even an anglicized name could not disguise one's looks or colour or the prevalent attitudes of the day towards an ethnic group that was expected to work in laundries or chop suey houses. The early 1900s was not the era in Canada for such a planned future, especially since Jack looked very Chinese even though he did not sport a queue and had an English sounding name. Mah Wing Chick, even with a new name like Jack Marvin, definitely still looked Chinese. Fortunately, another prospect opened for Jack, but in the meantime he contented himself with being invited to sing in various churches in Winnipeg.

This brief newspaper article appeared in the *Grande Prairie Herald* on January 3, 1930. It names some of the churches in Winnipeg where Jack sang during their worship services before he relocated to Grande Prairie from Winnipeg.

SINGING IN WINNIPEG CHURCHES

CHAPTER SIX

Grande Prairie Period (circa 1928 onwards)

Alaska Highway and Peace River Country
In the late twenties, the idea of the Alaska Highway was a germinating in the minds of politicians especially in the US. There was a developing concern among some of the world's powers about the Japanese and German expansionist tendencies that resulted in some quarters suggesting that a highway to Alaska through Canada would be a good idea strategically in case armies and supplies needed to get to and from the northwest coast quickly. Also at this time, the Peace River Country in Northern Alberta was beginning to be opened up, with crude roads and homesteads sprouting up in places where there were already some kind of access to other farms and small communities. The new province of Alberta was particularly anxious to continue opening up more of its provincial territory. Immigrants, especially from Europe, were lured by good homestead terms to this primitive landscape of prairie and forests, with its black fertile soil and gumbo. The building of the Northern Alberta Railway was also influential in bringing people north into various communities where roads were impassable or nonexistent. With the homesteads now beginning to harvest wheat and other grains and produce, elevators sprang up in the small towns

that needed the railway to send their grain to the rest of Canada and the world.

If there was any drawback to this land it would have been the so-called *gumbo* making automobile and horse and buggy travel totally frustrating in rainy weather.

Someone once remarked, "If I could find a use for gumbo, I would be a rich man."

Gumbo was the term used by residents of my day in the Peace River Country to describe the sticky mixture of rich black organic soil with clay and silty sand. Cars and wagons got thoroughly stuck in it on roads and fields. It would cling to your boots, making walking for little children rather fearful. I can vividly remember getting stuck in it once, wondering how I would extricate myself from it, and finally leaving my boots to walk barefoot in the mud, only retrieving my boots later when the ground dried up. My mother used to tell us stories of people she knew who got sucked up by quicksand. I thought that gumbo was kind of the same thing.

New Restaurant

At this critical time in his life, Jack Marvin was invited to start a restaurant in the small community of Grande Prairie in the Peace River Country, which would have been a major stopping place on the route to the Alaska Highway. A small airport had already begun to be built three miles from the town. Professional and commercial interests were soon expressing interest in the adventure of marketing in the remote but fertile lands and valleys of this beautiful, peaceful and beckoning area of Alberta. This adventure certainly appealed to Jack since his singing career was not going anywhere and he needed to find a different opportunity that would expand his financial resources more quickly than was happening in Winnipeg.

Jack was invited to move to Grande Prairie, where he received a certain amount of notoriety in the *Grande Prairie Herald* where they referred to him as "the singing Chinaman from Winnipeg" who would become the proprietor of a long awaited new restaurant called The Palace Café. We are not sure who would have contacted him for this venture. Perhaps it was the few Mah family members who might have already been there operating a laundry that was situated on the main street (later called Richmond Avenue). This laundry was called the Lee Laundry operated by the grandfather of Sam Mah whose father later became a cook and major kitchen operator in the Palace Café that Jack would soon launch.

Jack was the perfect person for such a venture. He was adventurous, liked a challenge, was organized, spoke excellent English, knew all the various jobs in a restaurant so that he could teach his employees, and had many links to countrymen and cousins. Grande Prairie was a peaceful, small pioneer prairie town with an interesting and promising future. It had not yet developed too much of a racial bias because everyone had a role to play there. Because of Jack's obvious talents and skills, he was well received and became a unique fixture in the town, singing in the local churches, choirs and musicals, playing golf on the primitive Richmond Hill golf course and later playing billiards in the men's-only pool hall.

Singing Chinaman

A few of the comments that appeared in the *Grande Prairie Herald*, spoke of his prominence as a baritone soloist and his restaurant, the Palace Café.

July, 1930: "The grand opening of the new food palace opened with a special dinner starting at 6 p.m. It will be much the largest in the North and fitted with all appointments as one sees only in large cities. In keeping with these ultra modern appointments a large neon sign of striking design combining three towers will adorn the front and will beckon the travellers and residents to the hospitality and service at all times paramount at the sign of the palace towers."

January 10, 1930 (St. Paul's United Church where the sermon by Rev. T.T. Reikie was about New Year's Resolutions) The headline in the paper reads: "Mr. J. Marvin, Formerly of Winnipeg, Delights With Two Fine Solos." The solos were Just For Today and My Task.

April 9, 1933 (the Grande Prairie symphony Concert): "The guest artist may not have been Stephen Kemalyan, but he was Jack Marvin whose trained Chinese baritone voice had thrilled audiences in the East before he had come to the Peace River country to settle and become one of the leading civic and cultural figures of Grande Prairie. His Bells of the Sea sung at the Sunday night concert was for years a favourite of his listeners."

May 25, 1933 (a concert by the Symphony Orchestra): "Jack Marvin, baritone, was splendid in his two songs, both of which are well fitted to his wide range - The Hills of Home and Bedouin."

September 10, 1936 (a dinner at the Palace café): "...about one hundred representatives of Grande Prairie and surrounding towns gathered in the Palace Café to honour Premier Aberhart at a banquet. Magnificent blooms from Jack Marvin's garden supplied a brilliant decorative note."

Western fare and Chinese Cuisine

Not only had Jack opened a restaurant that promised Western cuisine as well as Chinese, he had trained in the Winnipeg restaurants that catered to the cultural community with its more upscale tastes.

Although the following menu is too old a document to be a very good reproduction, it is an example of one of the first Christmas Dinners that the Palace Café offered to the citizens of Grande Prairie on December 19, 1928, even though its menu items are difficult for us to understand with our twenty-first century experience. It looks like Jack, or whoever did the ad, was trying to sound exotic.

The next menu, from December 1932 is a better example and certainly has a French sounding flair to it. The local restaurant fare catered to the food interests of the pioneers being mostly of European heritage. Obviously Jack had learned, in Winnipeg, how to elegantly describe what was offered so that it gave the restaurant an element of being first class.

It is reasonable to believe that perhaps, at first, Chinese food was not offered on any large scale to the local folk because it was too foreign for most, even though the sign on the windows of the Palace Café suggested that chop suey and noodle dishes were available.

JACK MARVIN

The management and staff of The Palace Café wish you the compliments of the season

PALACE CAFE

Christmas Menu

Fifty Cents Per Plate

APPETIZERS
Florida Basket
or
Gentlemen's Relish Canape

SOUP
Consomme Fidelina
Creme Tomato and Fairy Toast

FISH
Bouchee Oysters Supreme
Sturgeon Lake's Best and Citron

BOILED
Spiced Ham and Sauce Yorkshire
Boiled Capon-Hollander

ENTREES
Depression Chaser
Baton's Royaux of Game

ROAST
Choicest from the Manger
DinDonneaux (young turkey) and Wild Cranberry
Domestic Goose and Crabapple Jelly

SALAD AND VEGETABLE
Aspic of Lobster
Etouffe Celere   Olives
Pomme Victoria Parisienne
Spring Roots   Petite Pois

DESSERT
Season Plum Pudding and Hard Sauce
Icelander's Delight and Tender Touches
Green Apple Pie and Cheese
Hot Mince Pie   Boston Cream Pie
Christmas Cake   Imported Assorted

BEVERAGES
Tea   Cafe Noir   Chocolate   Milk

CHRISTMAS MENU

PHOTO OF BETTY IN FRONT OF PALACE CAFÉ

LATER CHRISTMAS MENU

Evelyn Marvin Millman

The real authentic Chinese cuisine had to be introduced gradually to a population that at first was suspicious of it. However, on the most important celebration days such as Christmas, New Years, and the Chinese New Year, the Chinese feasts in the back kitchens of all the local Chinese restaurants in the evenings of my day were sumptuous, exotic and delicious. But on other days, such as on our regular Sunday dinner after church, the menu had a decidedly European or Canadian flavour. The favourite of us children was veal cutlets or *finnan haddie* [smoked haddock]. We were not allowed to order Boston Cream Pie because it took too much time to make, but that was the only banned item.

Jack established many friends with his charming and winsome personality. He was not your typical Chinese immigrant who remained in the backgrounds of most towns and cities working his heart out during the day, then relieving the boredom of his evenings by gambling Mah Jong with his confreres into the wee hours of the morning. Their wives and children were not yet allowed to come to Canada, and so, with few exceptions, the Chinese community consisted of men only. Jack Marvin was different. He ran a fairly successful business. He learned to play golf. He fraternized with Caucasian business friends he met through the restaurant where a round oak table near the front door of his restaurant catered daily mid-morning and mid-afternoon coffee to anyone who thought they were someone in Grande Prairie.

The Grande Prairie Male Voice Choir
Jack joined the Grande Prairie Male Voice Choir and participated in the theatre productions and minstrel shows that played not only in the town but also in Dawson Creek on occasion. Otherwise these musical programs attracted people from all over the Peace River Country who lacked this kind of entertainment.

In a Grande Prairie musical drama production circa 1932. Jack is in top 2nd row, 2nd from the left with a painted black face. Beside him is the director of the production, Magistrate A. E. Galway, who was a prominent Grande Prairie citizen.

With his customers, Jack had a sense of humour as was evidenced by the two articles about his hunting exploits and the *special* dinners he was often called upon to prepare. Some of the delicacies that we, as a family, enjoyed were the many ducks shot by local farmers in the fall. Dad had a special way of preparing them that I have not tasted since—a combination of hoisin sauce, mandarin orange, and Chinese five spice. They were moist and delicious. He would prepare them in the restaurant kitchen and bring them home to his hungry brood. The local aboriginals at Sturgeon Lake Reserve also knew that they could unload their white fish catch at the restaurant. There again our family benefited.

Because our family was a unique mixture of Chinese and German, in later years we were privy to all the special Chinese events, and regularly made the tour of all four of the Chinese restaurants after hours to celebrate with everyone—the Royal Café, Joe's Corner Coffee Shop, the Donald Café and, of course, the Palace Café. Most of the single Chinese men had families back in China that could not be with them, so my siblings and I became surrogate children to these fellows, and of course, Dad loved to show us off whenever he got the chance.

At Christmas we received many toys and other gifts from these generous but lonely men. Our mother gave most of these gifts away

A. E. Galway, whose ancestors named and settled the Irish area known in history and song as Galway Bay, led his Male Voice Choir in their annual March 17 concert at the Capitol Theatre.

"Those present were privileged to hear an exceptionally fine program of Irish music . . . Father Maguire, chairman," reported the press March 21.

If the concert had a strong international touch it was because Jack Marvin, popular baritone, was a Chinese with a professionally-trained voice. "Jack Marvin sang two excellent solos 'Kathleen Mavourneen' and "Danny Boy". Mr. Marvin was in splendid voice and his solos were much enjoyed by the audience."

The high school orchestra under the direction of J. Jasbec played a quartet of numbers; Alice Adams "looked charming in her quaint little Irish costume" doing a tap dance; H. McHeffey "thrilled the audience with an exhibition of the difficult stair step dance"; Dr. Carlisle sang—"he is always popular"—as did Fred Lockyer. "Mr. Rodacker and J. Penson contributed two excellent duet guitar numbers . . ."

ONE OF MANY NEWSPAPER ARTICLES IN THE *GRANDE PRAIRIE HERALD* OF CONCERTS WHERE JACK SANG)

Police Confiscate Wild Goose as it Was to be Served

To have one's appetite all whetted up in anticipation for something for which one has a longing desire, and all at once to find that something has suddenly disappeared, would be considered the toughest kind of luck by the average healthy citizen.

Well, that is just what happened to a party of young men at Grande Prairie the other night.

Here is the story:

Jack Marvin, popular proprietor of the Palace Cafe, had been requested by a local boy who was putting on a little dinner party to cook a wild goose he had shot a few days before.

The goose was being cooked to a turn and was about to be served when policemen swooped down and confiscated the bird.

On Tuesday Jack Marvin appeared before Magistrate Galway and was fined $10 and costs for serving guests wild game without a permit. Jack has wired to the game commissioner for the necessary permit and is awaiting a reply.

The other game birds found on the premises were ordered to be returned to parties who presented the birds to the cafe.

The incident goes to show that sometimes there is a slip between goose and the lip.

Along The Trail
By J. B. YULE
Sept. 29, 1932

"THE ETERNAL FITNESS OF THINGS

The other morning Jack Marvin, manager of the Palace Cafe and well-known singer, sallied forth with several friends, primarily to hunt geese. Now, there is nothing particularly unusual about a man going on a goose hunt, but this time Jack differed from many of the local nimrods in that he was dressed for the occasion, from long boots, hunting jacket, to the cap.

The popular singer and restaurant man did not bag any geese, but he was successful in getting several mallards and one teal.

Ordinarily, Jack explained, he would just go out clad in ordinary clothes, but when it came to shooting the lordly goose that was a different matter and should be done according to Hoyle. A man can go, said Jack, to a vaudeville show in his business suit, but the opera calls for full dress.

Jack, who managed Bob Rogers' commissary department for a number of years, is a stickler for the "eternal fitness of things" and would no more think of going to hunt geese clad in ordinary garb than he would think of going before an audience clad in overalls.

Jack informed the writer that he is not discouraged and will continue to occupy "the pits" until he gets at least one goose. All this, he said, he would do dressed in a garb befitting the occasion.

* * *

HUMOUROUS NEWSPAPER ARTICLES

Evelyn Marvin Millman

because, after all, what does one do with twenty dolls or twenty boxes of Pot of Gold chocolates. It was an exciting time for us. However, when we started going to school the racial biases began to appear, especially for my brothers, although we all endured a little of it. Boys being boys, our brothers would enter into minor scraps and fights with those who didn't know any better. Some of these hostilities and animosities lasted for years, but on the whole they didn't amount to much worth getting upset about.

We girls shrugged off the racial slurs as coming from ignorant kids that we couldn't be bothered with. When we hear about modern day bullying that sometimes has disastrous consequences, I am glad we lived at that time in our history. Mostly I would say that all four of us grew up with good self-esteem and did well in school. We had good family relationships with our mother's family, were respected in our church and, as I mentioned earlier, felt we were the surrogate children of all the Chinese men in the various Chinese cafés and shops in town. Both our parents had a certain stature in the community, and that helped too.

A Summer Prank c. 1948
Unfortunately, one warm summer night, a gang of kids must have raided our parents' market garden because plants were pulled up and debris littered the ground the next morning. There was a lot of evidence that there were quite a few in the group because of the footprints in the loose dirt and the amount of damage. We didn't know who did this, but what was there for us to do?

Many times, when we kids were working in the gardens during the summer holidays, we would make sandwiches by putting the washed vegetables into a lettuce leaf and eating our creation. Obviously the culprits came from families whose moms or dads didn't plant peas and lettuce and beans and carrots in their gardens like we were used to. For us there was nothing better to eat than fresh vegetables taken directly out of the ground. Freshly shelled peas were our favourites, and Mom would often have to tell us to quit eating all the peas.

In those days there was no such thing as fast food outlets where you could buy a hamburger or a hotdog laden with relish and mustard during warm summer evenings. I suppose a garden ripe for the picking was a good target for youngsters, and ours was close to town but secluded and far enough from town that you might not get caught.

Whoever did this damage didn't realize how hard everyone in our family worked to get our produce to the point of harvesting—after plowing the fields, planting the seeds, weeding the rows, watering the plants, picking and shelling the peas, picking and canning the beans, pulling out the carrots, lettuce, onions for washing and then doing the canning for the winter months or putting the produce into bunches and crates for distribution to the local stores for their customers. This represented hours and hours of child labor that many of our peers might not have had to do.

Rumours began to circulate in our small town, but we soon forgot the disaster and never heard who might have done this damage. About twenty-five years later, when we attended a Grande Prairie High School Reunion where everyone was relating their high school exploits and their teenage shenanigans, the truth began to come out even though I had completely forgotten the episode. One of my classmates who was involved in the garden raid, thinking I knew the whole story, rather shamefully told me what actually happened after the raid. If my memory is accurate someone got caught and others squealed to their parents who then took the appropriate action that good parents usually do. In the meantime, Dad casually reported the damage to his good friend Judge Galway, the local magistrate, who called together all of the culprits that he could discover and charged them each a dollar which they were to give to Mr. Marvin. They were also to apologize personally to him for what they had done and then report back to the judge.

If my siblings were aware of this story, I certainly was not. I like to think that Dad never told me about it because most of the culprits were from my school class. He thought that it might be difficult for me in the classroom, but I was naively unaware and never even gave it a second thought or concern.

CHAPTER SEVEN

Elizabeth Wiedeman's Family Immigration (1912)

Like many of our relationships in life, including that of our mom and dad's, chance and circumstance play a major part in shaping the outcome. In Jack and Betty's lives, the chance encounters and desperate circumstances that befell two unique people in the early years of the twentieth century did indeed shape their future and that of their children.

Our mother, like most Elizabeths of the day, was known by a shortened version of her name—in her case, she was known Betty to everyone. She first met Jack when she went to work in his restaurant after her father had died and the family had moved to Grande Prairie.

"Betty is the best waitress we've ever had in our restaurant," I would often hear Dad say to folks who visited our home.

Immigration from Russia

Betty's family were new German immigrants from the Mennonite colony of Nue York near what was then Ekaterinoslav, Russia [today Dnipro, Ukraine]. In 1912 when Betty was two years old and her younger brother Alexander was only one, their parents decided to come to Canada. The political situation in Russia was becoming dangerous and tenuous for the German population especially anyone with

BETTY'S PARENTS

Mennonite affiliations. Maria (Mary) Janzen, Betty's mother, was from the German Mennonite community. Wilhelm (William) Wiedeman, Mary's husband was from the German Lutheran community.

Betty's German forefathers were expert farmers and machinists making them good candidates to immigrate to Russia during Catherine the Great's reign—indeed Ekaterinoslav was named for her. Catherine was searching in Germany, Poland, and Holland for people with these capabilities to infiltrate the southern fertile prairie land of Russia to teach their skills to the native Russians. It didn't turn out quite as expected. It was to be expected that, because the immigrants were a very large group, they would bring their culture and religion with them.

At the time, the region was quite unproductive in the hands of the native population there. The natives were not as industrious as the new immigrants and weren't always interested in learning their skills, ending up being merely servants and farmhands while the new immigrants became wealthy and exclusive. The immigrants did not help matters any when they would not integrate into the Russian community but built their own churches, schools, stores, factories and hospitals and other institutions so that their languages and religions would be preserved. They would not allow their adult children to mix or intermarry with the Russians. In the German community especially, this led to the practice of shunning and the ostracizing anyone who did not obey their family's religious and cultural policies. And the exclusivity of the immigrant population eventually led to political friction and jealousies, causing hostilities among the native Russians in the early decades of the twentieth century. This gradually escalated to such an extent that, during the Bolshevik Revolution, many Germans were killed protecting their properties or were forced to flee to safer nations like Canada. There was also growing animosity towards Russia's ruling imperial family and an impending proletariat uprising that eventually led to a Marxist communist government. The consequences of these changes in the texture of the Russian nation's politics and economics resulted in untold atrocities and bloodshed that reverberates to this day.

Bolshevik Upheaval

In the chaos and turmoil, one of the Wiedeman brothers was sent to a camp north of Moscow in the uprising. His pregnant wife, with three children in tow, hitched their horses onto a wagon and attempted to find and join him there in the middle of winter. It is not known what happened to any of them. Two of the other Wiedeman brothers made a decision to find a safe haven for their families in the south of Manitoba where Canada was settling a group of German immigrants, many of whom were of the Mennonite faith. With encouragement from these two brothers, William and Mary subsequently made the same decision and followed them to the farms of Manitoba. Mary's family also followed, settling in both Manitoba and in the Abbottsford area in British Columbia.

WIEDEMAN MEN IN RUSSIA

BABY BETTY

Betty was born into this uncertainty and tension in the Mennonite community of Neu York in 1910.

When her family's life flowed to southern Manitoba her father, William Wiedeman, tried to keep the body and soul of his family together as a farmhand on homesteads during some of the worst dust storms, droughts, grasshoppers and blizzards that Manitoba has ever endured in the years preceding the Great Depression of the early thirties. He and his growing

Evelyn Marvin Millman

MAP OF UKRAINE IN RUSSIA
SHOWING AREA OF BETTY'S PARENTS BIRTHPLACE CIRCLED IN BLACK.

family moved through several communities and farms during the next few years such as Morden, Myrtle, Plum Coulee and Winkler. Mary Janzen had come from a wealthy Mennonite farming community in Russia and loved the agricultural lifestyle that she enjoyed there. William's background and job in Russia was in machining and building farm implements for the growing industrialization of the agricultural economy that was sweeping all of the emerging economies of the world.

PHOTO OF EARLY FARM IN MANITOBA WHERE WILLIAM WORKED AS A FARMHAND

William and Mary's move to the Peace River Country
What follows are excerpts of an interview Nieta later had with her older sister, Suzanne (Susan), in June of 1996. Nieta was the youngest of thirteen children of Mary and William. Betty was the oldest and Susan was in the middle.

"Dad had heard of homestead land in the Peace River Country that could be his if he *proved it up* for five years."

Proving it up meant clearing the trees and vegetation from the land so that crops could be planted. In the twenties and thirties, this was a back-breaking task. It was done with a team of horses or even just one horse depending on the wealth of the person applying for the land.

Stones and vegetation needed to be cleared out with a stone boat—a crude raft-like structure made of logs that slid along the ground. It was hooked up to the horses and pulled over the terrain and loaded with either rocks or discarded trees and bushes. The horses would be hooked up to the trees pulling them and their root systems out with great effort. Often when travelling past land that has been cleared, one can see piles of rocks on the side of the farm as well as piles of fallen trees and bushes left to rot in time or be burned when it is safe to do so. With Mary's encouragement, William finally secured a homestead near the small community of Lymburn, Alberta, several miles from the settlement towns of Hythe and Beaverlodge, about forty miles northwest of Grande Prairie.

"Applying and getting the land, Dad came ahead of the family and organized the homestead details and land. He worked in Grande Prairie for a year in a sawmill as a carpenter, and during that time he sent for the family. They traveled across the country by train to Grande Prairie where they all stayed in the Immigration Hall until the home was ready for them and until Dad got enough money together to buy two horses, cows and chickens. When they were ready, the animals were put on a boxcar and sent to Lymburn.

"In the meantime, Dad, Alex, and Bill had built a house of logs on the homestead land. It didn't have a floor that first winter because the government said they would provide the sawmill facility if the home-steaders applied before the end of the year and then would cut the trees and let them dry to be cut in the summer. However, that next summer a forest fire burned all the wood and the trees that the home-steaders had cut down for drying. This meant another winter without a floor in the house. The following spring, they again cut their trees, dried them, and had them cut into timber for the floor."

By this time, the Wiedeman family had increased to twelve, and a thirteenth child, Nieta, was born on the homestead in 1933. Though she was my kid sister, she would end up being more like a sister to Betty's kids due to her age."

WIEDEMAN FAMILY OF 12 CHILDREN

William Wiedeman's Death

As I mentioned, in Russia, William Wiedeman and his brothers were machinists. Farming was not in their blood to the same extent as it was in Mary's. She had worked in the farms and homes of wealthy Mennonite families and longed to build the same experience here in Canada. However, after a few years, just when it looked like the family was finally feeling at home on their homestead, tragedy struck. William had an accident near the homestead when he took his team of horses and wagon out to get feed for them from a nearby farmer during a pouring rain and extremely muddy conditions.

"They were crossing a rain swollen river to get to a farmer who would sell them grain. When he was part way over the bridge, it was swept away by the rising flood. Dad and his team hung on to the edge of the bank but were unable to pull themselves up to the land. He yelled and yelled, and fortunately, the next morning, the farmer and his men were just on their way out to their fields when they heard Dad. They quickly got their horses and pulled them up the bank.

Evelyn Marvin Millman

Because Dad had been in the water so long, he had become chilled and cold (probably hypoothermia) and became sick. He did not feel well for a week or two, and the following Sunday he had a stroke while his family were at a church picnic and while he was looking after the new baby, six-month-old Nieta.

"When his family returned home, they attempted to get a doctor, but because of the muddy roads the doctor could not get there. So the RCMP constable for Hythe told Alex, the oldest son, that if he could get Dad to a point on the road where a car could get to them, he would take Dad to the hospital in Grande Prairie. Mary with her two sons, Alex and Bill, took Dad on their horse drawn wagon for a long and rough ride. Then the RCMP constable took Dad along with Mom to the hospital in Grande Prairie, where he died July 7, 1933, on the first night. While Mom was in town she stayed with her daughter, Mary, who was working as a maid there."

"After Dad's death, Mom went back to the homestead with her children and took care of the crops and whatever else they had to care for. She knew that Jake, who was quite crippled with polio at a young age,

YOUTHFUL GRANDMA WIEDEMAN

would need to be close to a school. So she and the family made a heartbreaking decision to move to Grande Prairie. They moved into a small home in the Bear Creek flats that brothers Henry and John began to enlarge and remodel to accommodate everyone. There were lots of large trees and space in the yard for a large garden."

See Appendix E

Move to Grande Prairie from the Homestead

What a heartbreaking decision for a recently widowed mother to leave the homestead that they had all worked so hard to clear and build! In Grande Prairie, it was possible for the older children to find work to keep the family together and possible to get short-term government relief while they looked for work. Mary was able to rent a small home in the Bear Creek Flats. It was no luxurious dwelling, but it did provide shelter and a chance to keep the family together in one place no matter how crowded. The building was an unpainted simple structure with a dugout cellar and an attic.

It was situated in the flats of a beautiful valley along Bear Creek that ran through the western part of the town. Of course, there was no running water except for the running that the boys might have had to do to get water from some other sources like the neighbour's well. In addition to no indoor plumbing, there was no electricity, telephone, or furnace at first—just the bare essentials that other pioneer families also endured during the first few decades of the twentieth century's in similar small towns and farms. The floors were wooden planks, and to keep the house better insulated against the cold winters, sod and dirt had to be shovelled against the outer walls.

Despite the meagre amenities, at least it housed the entire family—even though the boys at first all slept on mattresses or straw ticks on the floor in the one upper attic room. They had brought along their homestead wooden furniture and woollen patchwork quilts made from old coats. Everything usable was recycled. The yard had two fairly large vegetable gardens, one of which was a sunken garden that got flooded sometimes in the spring from the adjoining creek.

Eventually the older boys got odd jobs in the town, and the older girls worked as cleaning ladies in some of the wealthier homes—as did Betty, who later secured a job as a waitress in Jack's restaurant that was to change her life.

CHAPTER EIGHT

Marriage and New Family

Jack and Betty's courtship was cemented during some of the romantic musicals of that day such as *Show Boat* and *Rosemarie* in the local Capital movie theatre featuring such current famous singers as Jeannette MacDonald and Nelson Eddy. Dad's musical repertoire of love songs from that era also portray his romantic nature. Despite the vast difference in their ethnic cultures and an age gap of almost twenty-three years, the inevitable happened. Jack and Betty fell in love and finally married when it looked like a baby was on the way.

In the thirties a baby born out of wedlock was a personal disgrace so most women in this situation would go away from the community to have the baby, give the baby up for adoption, or make an attempt to have an abortion—sometimes with fatal consequences. As told to me by my mother many years later, she went to the small town of Pouce Coupe, near Dawson Creek, close to the border of British Columbia. That is where Jack found her. He persuaded her to return to Grande Prairie because he loved her and wanted to marry her We cannot imagine the heartache that many women suffered in. those days when faced with making such momentous decisions about a premarital pregnancy. In our modern age, our Canadian society has become more charitable and understanding, and there are organizations that help women face these issues with support and counselling.

MARVIN--WIEDMANN

A quiet wedding took place at the Presbyterian manse on Tuesday evening, October 17, when Miss Betty Weidmann, eldest daughter of Mrs. Weidmann of Lymburn and the late William Weidmann became the bride of Jack Marvin, the well known restaurateur.

The ceremony was preformed by the Rev. E. A. Wright and was witnessed by Miss Mary Weidmann, sister of the bride, Mrs. M. E. Brewer and Joe Putters.

The bride was becomingly gowned in a wine colored creation trimmed with white beading shoes and stockings to match.

Wedding Bells

MARVIN-WEIDMAN

Jack Marvin, proprietor of the Palace Cafe and well known singer, and Miss Betty Wiedman were united in marriage at the Presbyterian manse on Tuesday evening last. Rev. E. A. Wright performed the ceremony.

• • • •

WEDDING ANNOUNCEMENTS

Evelyn Marvin Millman

The Wedding

Their marriage was not exactly an acceptable occurrence in those days, and it took some time before the family and the community got used to it. First of all, Betty's very German family viewed this improbable union with great dismay in the beginning. Also this did not sit well with her local Baptist church whose deacons would not allow their minister, the Reverend Waterman, to marry them, more probably because of the interracial overtones of a marital union that they had never encountered before.

The Reverend Waterman wanted badly to marry Jack and Betty, for he liked Betty and her character and he knew Jack from his respected restaurant business. However, they finally tied the knot in a small wedding in the local Presbyterian Church with a Jewish friend, Joe Putters, as best man and Betty's sister, Mary, as bridesmaid. Joe Putters' German housekeeper, Evelyn Brewster, who later became Putter's wife, also attended the wedding ceremony and eventually the new baby girl was named after her. In our present era, this marriage must now seem quite usual. At that time, however, it was anything but. Furthermore, Joe Putters and Evelyn Brewster's relationship—at a time when Jews in Germany and other parts of the world were facing discrimination of a different sort by the German Nazis—must have also seemed like a rather unique and gutsy experience.

If Jack and Betty's marriage seemed unusual or even unnatural to most folks at the time, their offspring like to think of it as an enlightened happening by two independent individuals who had the courage to proceed with their plans and their love for each other. Jack had become quite well known in Grande Prairie for running a good restaurant business and for his excellent baritone voice, which he put to good advantage by singing in local churches and in the local choirs and musical shows. Betty was well known for her industrious and hardworking nature and the good friends she had developed in her church, in the restaurant, and in the community, and especially for the way she cared for and helped her mother and siblings at a difficult time.

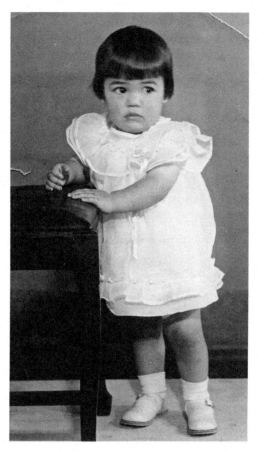

FIRSTBORN EVELYN

Arrival of Grand Children

The community and family soon adapted to this new marital union and to the children that were soon born, especially because Jack was very kind to Betty's family, giving them boxes of fruit and food from the food wholesales that he had access to—and turkeys at Christmas and New Year's. The four children were well received and coddled by all the new aunts and uncles and by Betty's mother, now Grandma Wiedeman. These were her first grandchildren. If anything, at first the children were quite on display as the community was curious to see what such a marital union would produce, how the children would behave, and how they would eventually do in school. Today, as we all now know, this seems quite ridiculous as mixed marriages are so common and the offspring of such unions are the same as any others.

A Chinese Bachelor

Although Betty didn't know it at the time, she was marrying a Chinese bachelor of some forty-five years. Jack was the same age as Mary, now mother-in-law, and, therefore, a full generation ahead of his new bride. Betty was twenty-three years old, and the prospect of some financial security with a man who *looked* her age must have seemed quite promising and attractive at that time during the middle of the Great Depression. But Jack had lived on his own and left to his own devices since arriving in Canada and had not learned the intricacies of nurturing a family or building a home since he had left his own family at such a young age. His life was that of a bachelor, and at his age, he found it difficult to change. Betty soon learned to adapt to Jack's independence, and indeed Jack relished the fact that he finally had a family. He became a pseudo patron immersed in a small way in Betty's large family of brothers and sisters—a family that he never had in Canada. It was a good feeling for him. Betty, on the other hand, had to find her own way in the marriage while her husband did all the things he had done before without regard for the fact he had a wife at home who now had to care for her growing family of four children, Evelyn, Jack Jr., Eva and Billy.

An Unique Woman

Betty Wiedeman was truly unique. She was the oldest of thirteen children and had, early on, learned how to be responsible, to care for younger siblings, to do a man's hard work on the farms, and to eventually provide assistance to her devastated family after her father died. She was resourceful and independent, making decisions about her young family while her husband worked and played at his various community ventures.

YOUNG FAMILY

Evelyn Marvin Millman

She was devout in her Christian faith and worked tirelessly in her church teaching Sunday School and being active in the Women's Mission Circle. At times she even worked at the restaurant when help was hard to find or when workers did not meet Jack's specifications and demands. She was always his best waitress. Along with her mother, Betty canned vegetables and summer fruit and chickens for the long winter months that were the norm for Grande Prairie. She sewed the clothes for all her brood as well as the white shirts Jack wore in the restaurant. In her few leisure hours, she embroidered, crocheted, tatted and knitted sweaters, scarves and socks. There was never a moment to lose or to be idle. Her kids saw to that with their activities, energies, and appetites. There was no time for them to be coddled, babied, spoiled, or favoured either. Getting a fever or flu or the measles was rather wonderful if you could manage it because you got rarities like tomato juice or orange juice and could stay in bed for a day or so, but you dared not expect much else.

While Betty was rearing her family, Jack was making a great living, but while money was made easily it was also spent easily. I had a saying that I often repeated to others when I grew older.

"When Dad had money he spent it. When he didn't have money he didn't spend it."

It was as simple as that. We children didn't seem to notice the difference, and as far as I know, it never became an issue in our home. Mom had her own way of making money and was kind of independent of Dad.

Of his mother, Jack Jr. used to say that she was the hardest working lady he had ever known or come in contact with during his life. Bill also says *Amen* to that because both of these sons experienced her leadership and industrious, tireless ethic on the farm. Mom never grumbled or complained about her hard life because it was the norm for most other families at that time. Most of the time Dad didn't have money to spend on his family that we knew of, and this was when Mom had to become an entrepreneur of sorts. In this way, having or not having money really never was an issue until we got older. Then we all had to be left to our own devices to make ends meet or to finance our needs and our future education. We never expected our parents to help us get through university or pay our bills while getting a career. It was extremely hard work to live in poverty while trying to get an education, especially since none of us lived at home. It usually meant working at a job or two while trying to attend classes and studying for exams. It meant borrowing money from friends and family members in an era when student loans were not yet established as a means of paying for an education. If your family had the financial means, you could choose any option at university that you had your heart set on if you also had the grades for your choice. Career options for girls at that time were also limited—nursing, teaching, secretarial, period. Jobs for girls were limited, and the remuneration for girls in those jobs couldn't compare with what the boys could make doing the same thing. Many things have changed in our country over the past eight decades thanks to the women who fought for more equality over the course of my lifetime.

CHAPTER NINE

Travels

Jack bought his first car—a Model A Ford, I think—shortly before or after his marriage. Usually once or twice a year Jack and Betty drove the twelve hour or more drive to Edmonton where Betty's sister Helen and her husband, Fred Carlson, lived at 9650 - 107 Avenue. Depending on the season, sometimes this twelve- to fourteen-hour trip would take two to three days if the Lesser Slave Lake was flooding or if the rains had made the dirt and gravel roads impassable.

They would often have to join other travellers along the way, cutting down small trees to make a so-called *corduroy road*. This was a road where the trees were laid across the gumbo or muskeg so that cars could traverse the boggy parts. Looking at the following photo, I can't remember what this was like.

CORDUROY ROAD

Although I was too young to remember all the details of these incidents, we children would always accompany our parents on these trips. It would have been quite exciting for us as preschool children at first to stand up in the car to watch all these proceedings. We never thought to ask, "Are we there yet?" because there was too much excitement along the road. Even in 1952 when my parents took me to College in Calgary, the seven-mile hill west of Valleyview and east of Grande Prairie was so muddy and full of ruts after a rain that, when you were at the top of the hill looking down the seven-mile stretch towards the town of Valleyview, you would have a view of about fifty cars and trucks stuck in the gumbo at various places on the hill. The occupants of each car would get out and push out the ones ahead of them so they could then traverse the rest of the stretch. If they got mired in the mud again the whole procedure would be repeated until everyone was safely out. This took us about five hours to get to better road. The miracle of this common procedure in the late thirties was that it was expected and no one had a fit about not getting to where they were going in record time. The thought was, for instance, *I wonder if we can make it to Edmonton in twelve hours this time* because it was expected that there would be something along the primitive road to hinder one's progress.

Singing at First Baptist Church, Edmonton

On most trips to Edmonton, Jack was invited by Mrs. Barber-Smith, the English organist and choir director at First Baptist Church, to sing solos in her downtown church. At that time this grand old church was directly southwest of the Eaton store on 102nd Avenue and 102nd Street. First Baptist was a more liberal church than most Baptist churches at that time with respect to its inclusion of ethnic groups who might be shunned by others. It became renowned for allowing Paul Robeson, the famous Afro-American baritone, to sing in their worship service during the early forties when he travelled through Edmonton on a concert tour. However, Robeson was not allowed to give a concert in Edmonton because of his colour—but also because he was suspected of being a communist. As a preschool child, I recall sitting in the dark oak pews in the front row of the church with my mother and Aunt Helen as Dad sang in the oak-lined choir loft of that elegant First Baptist Church. That church was later replaced by a parking lot and relocated to 109th Street where a much less elegant structure was built—unfortunately the victim of redevelopment elsewhere. Today the Edmonton downtown YMCA occupies the same spot where the original church stood.

While Jack did not have the same famous stature as Robeson, it was still a great incitement for Jack to encourage his family to attend the McLaurin Baptist Church in Grande Prairie, where Betty attended, even though he was not allowed to sing there as he did at the United and Presbyterian churches in Grande Prairie because he was a smoker. It was considered one of many sins that the church prohibited for its members. However, Jack was not one to harbour grudges about a small thing like this and encouraged his children to attend church with their mother. Jack was never a religious person, but he was very much a spiritual man who would repeat the sayings of Confucius and lots of Christian sayings when he wanted us to know how to behave. One incident happened when I was a teenager practicing at the church for a Christmas program with some rather unruly teenagers who were giggling and causing a stir. It was the middle of winter, and Dad had agreed to pick me up by car on a very cold night. Standing at the back of the church waiting for me while we continued to practice, he couldn't stand the kibitzing any longer.

"This is the House of the Lord, and you should act accordingly with more respect than I am witnessing here," said Dad. "Now get on with it!"

I was sitting at the piano accompanying the choir and was totally dumbfounded to hear my Dad, a man I didn't think was the least bit religious let alone Christian, angrily blurt that out. There was a moment of great hush, and I wanted to crawl under the pew with embarrassment in front of my peers. Needless to say, we proceeded with our practice in short but calm order.

Sunday Dinners and a Singing Dad

One of the incitements for us to accompany Mom to church was that after church we could order anything we wanted from the menu in Dad's restaurant—everything that is except the Boston Cream Pie. This dinner with Dad was a weekly occurrence for us and was the only meal, apart from special occasions, we ever ate with him.

Among his Chinese confreres in the restaurants, and unbeknownst to our family, Jack was respectfully known among them as *the little Christian*—this according to Sam Mah, one of our distant cousins who came to Canada in 1949 and worked in Dad's restaurant. Knowing this now, it seems quite reasonable to me since he sang his musical renditions in the churches and to his friends with such passion and religious fervour in a way he never expressed verbally to his family. Since I was usually Dad's pianist in my teens, I would often see folks wiping the tears from their eyes as he sang. He had quite a good repertoire of both religious songs and secular ones—pieces like "Bless This House", "The Lord's Prayer", "The Holy City", and "Trees", "Kathleen Mavourneen", "Danny Boy", and "If I Were King Of Ireland" to name a few selections that are no longer popular.

One thing Dad did was sing and not scream or yell as seems to be the vogue today. He could project his powerful voice in a large hall without benefit of loud speakers, microphones, or other modern day sound paraphernalia. Alternatively, he could also sing in a soft gentle voice with the utmost clarity. This ability showed how well he had been trained earlier in his Winnipeg days. He sang well into his late sixties, but one day, when he was singing in a concert at the local theatre with me at the piano, he faltered slightly in his pitch when he was doing a rendition of "Neapolitan Nights." Perhaps it was the distance that the piano and I were from him, but I knew then that he was nearing the end of a great singing sensation for a Chinese immigrant boy. I think he knew it too, and rather than suffer the embarrassment of singing publicly any further, he sang alone at home, sometimes with me at the piano on my brief visits back to my home town.

When I ponder this now, I experience a great feeling of sadness at the tragedy of my Dad not being able to fully utilize his talent more publicly in a way that could have given him greater satisfaction in his life in Canada. Singing was his great obsession. Everything else was a filler to make a living or to make friends. In his later senior years, he took up other activities that filled this vacant space. He became an expert billiard player in the local pool hall, outplaying most of his opponents.

Today as I ponder Dad's singing life, I am reminded of him and his excellent baritone voice when I hear famous singers like Andrea Bocelli sing so beautifully. Dad's voice had a resonance that is no longer necessary in modern singers be they rock stars or other popular recording artists with the ever present luxury of microphones and sound systems that project their voices over the crowd to the farthest reaches of the venues in which they appear. Although Bocelli is a tenor and Dad was a baritone, they were similar in the way they clearly articulated their words and phrases, allowing their final notes and words to fade away with the utmost reluctance and clarity and breath control. This is the sign of a true musical artist. Bocelli is a blind man, and when you don't have your eyesight, you pay great attention to the small nuances of the sound you produce and how you produce it. You are not distracted by the audience or the surroundings. You can just be immersed in the music and what it means to you as a singer. That is exactly how Jack sang. He closed his eyes and sang from the depths of his heart. If he were living today, without the racism he experienced in his day, he could have become a very unusual singing sensation as he was then in the small town of Grande Prairie.

CHAPTER TEN

Betty Wiedeman's Family

Each of Grandma and Grandpa Wiedeman's children played their part in weaving the fabric of our nation, some in the armed forces during World War II, some in raising families and keeping the home fires burning waiting for their return, some in construction, some in various service industries and businesses, but all contributing according to their talents and skills and educations.

BETTY IN FRONT OF LOG HOME

Elizabeth (Betty) – born April 7, 1910

Betty was the oldest of thirteen siblings consisting of seven brothers and five sisters. Before the family moved to Alberta, Betty was old enough to work as a housemaid to help with the family finances. She worked for a short while in Winnipeg where she was employed by quite a wealthy family. We do not know much about this episode in her life except her story of being quite unaccustomed to the accoutrements that wealth displays. She was a good housekeeper—we know *that*—but one day she set the sterling silver tea service on the back of the stove in much the same way one would do with a stainless steel pot. After several hours of attending to other duties she returned to the kitchen to witness the sad state of the tea service and tray. Not being used to the care of expensive sterling silver dishes she was distraught to see that the heat of the stove had caused the tea service to start melting and was beginning to crumple like a car in a bad accident. She did not last long enough there to see whether the tea service could be returned to its original state, or whether it was unsalvageable, or whether she could expect a recommendation for another job. Thus ended her career in the big city, and she went back to join her family on one of the Manitoba farms, probably much to her mother's happiness because she could now help with the growing brood of siblings that Grandma and Grandpa Wiedeman seemed to be having.

During her life, Betty learned to be flexible and to change with any circumstances that came her way. Later this was a necessity if she was married to Jack. She loved to travel with Dad and had not been afraid to venture out into the wider world of travels by herself after Dad died. She travelled alone to the Netherlands to visit Jack Jr. and family when Jack was stationed in The Hague and working on projects in Rotterdam. She would have gone to Pakistan too, when both Bill and Jack worked on the Tarbela Dam project there in the seventies near Rawalpindi, if all of us hadn't put our collective feet down about it. However, after Jack moved to Fort Erie and Houston, and Bill moved to Montreal and Oregon, she never hesitated one moment to visit them wherever they were.

After the hard work of the family farm life was over, Betty had gotten jobs in hospitals and was always very active in the churches she attended. After her husband's death, she moved herself to various apartments in Edmonton on her own just as she had moved the family from one house to the other on her own devices in Grande Prairie. She knew a thing or two about the hard life that her siblings might not have known about and made sure they became aware of it.

Uncle Alex - born December 14, 1911

Next in line to Betty was Alexander, Alex for short. He was a year younger than Betty and like his older sister was born in Russia. He grew up to be a giant of a man with red hair and beard like his dad.

UNCLE ALEX

Alex got several jobs around town doing carpenter work and in the north on the Alaska Highway shortly after the family moved to Grande Prairie from the homestead. We only saw him occasionally. In our youthful eyes, he seemed like a gentle giant that we respected but didn't get too close to. He served in the Canadian Navy on a warship during World War II with his brother Henry.

I was in London, Ontario, once in the early nineties to visit a new pipe organ that was being built there—and to visit one of my umbrella dealers—so I took the opportunity to visit my Uncle Alex whom I rarely saw. At the time he was in a Veteran's hospital there. His legs had been amputated because of gangrene, and he was in a wheelchair. While working in the cold north he had contracted gangrene in his legs which became infected further in his senior years. He had collected all his photos of our family to give me on my visit, so in his senior years he must have sensed that his life was coming to an end. He related the following story to me with tears in his eyes and a wholesome infectious laugh that emanated from somewhere inside of him and flowed to everyone else who was in earshot.

"I didn't get home very often, but on one of my infrequent visits, I was relaxing in the big easy chair in front of the window of my mother's house where I had a view of the hill in front. Your mother used to bring you kids to Grandma's house at least once a week. The last leg of your walk was down that hill in front of our house. I called to everyone in the house at the time...

"Baton down the hatches. Here come the Marvin brats."

Evelyn Marvin Millman

"With Betty following, all four of you little urchins came running down the hill at top speed right through the front door where I was sitting with one foot on top of the other. Obviously you all weren't expecting to see me, maybe Jake or Nieta or Grandma but not me. You all stopped short in utter disbelief at the sight of me with my red hair and red beard and especially my huge feet. With a sort of innocent childish shock on your faces all four of you stood there examining my huge body for a brief moment. Then in a state of awed but frightened quiet one of you whispered, "What big feet he has!""

Uncle Alex found it difficult to coherently relate this story to me as he remembered the moment so long ago when he was a young man. He was laughing so hard, he cried. All the rest of us surrounding him, his wife Doris, the nurses and the other patients, were so moved by what he said and by his infectious laughter as he tried so hard to tell us this story that we were joining him in laughter too while holding our sides and wiping our eyes. What a precious moment for all of us! He died shortly after, and I was so grateful that I had made this chance to hear a story I was unaware of. I think he would have been a good father, but he and his wife never had any children.

Aunt Mary – born January 5, 1914

Aunt Mary was born two years later in Roland, Manitoba. She always seemed to be quite fragile and was in a tuberculosis sanatorium for a year. She was Betty's bridesmaid when Betty and Jack got married in 1933. She later moved to Ontario during the war years where she had a job as a seamstress in a shoe factory. She later married Alfred Barre and lived in Trenton, Ontario, until her death. She and Alfred adopted two children, Gwen and David. We really didn't have a chance to know Aunt Mary and her family very well because they lived

AUNT MARY WITH
HUSBAND ALFRED BARRE

in eastern Ontario where we never went because it was too far to take all of our family, but she and Uncle Alfred came to Edmonton once to stay with Aunt Helen at which time we also came to the city to visit them. Their children were very young at the time, and we never had a chance to get to know them as they grew up and finally had families of their own.

Aunt Helen – born October 31, 1915

AUNT HELEN

Aunt Helen was also born in Roland, Manitoba, a year after Mary. Because Helen eventually lived in Edmonton, we got to know her well. Dad quite liked her because she was so spirited and candid and was a good cook. Because of her well known outspoken nature, we always knew where we stood with her. She would scold you for making too much noise or for running around her well-kept home without restraint or for putting too much water in the claw-foot tub we all would bathe in after our long, dusty journey from Grande Prairie. Our idea of a bath at that time was a two-foot square galvanized tub heated on the stove with water that we either melted from snow in winter, or that in summer was delivered to the huge water barrel inside the kitchen by the man we called the *waterman*. He came to our house twice a week and filled up our barrel. Then one after the other we would all bathe in the same water. I can hardly bear the thought of it now, but at that time we were too small to care. So arriving at Aunt Helen's house was such a treat. She would fill up her big bathtub and in all four of us would go. It seemed to us to be heaven itself to have so much water in the tub, and we didn't mind that she would not let us run around the house until we had that bath.

Besides being a good cook, she was also a great seamstress and loved to make stuffed animals for us that would put the current *stuffie* manufacturers to shame. The Bambi deer that she made were complete with little tiny ears, a tiny puff ball for a tail, and thin stuffed legs wired inside for support. I can remember receiving a huge box at Christmas time with all manner of animals that she and Aunt Suzanne (Susan) had made for us. What a treat for the little rascals that we were in our preschool years!

For all her scolding, we knew that Aunt Helen loved little children because she was always looking after somebody's child. Maybe it was because she had lost her own baby in infancy several years earlier and having children around gave her some comfort for her loss. Uncle Fred, her husband, was a most patient man. I'm sure that Aunt Helen made his life exciting and interesting. At Aunt Helen's we certainly were on our best behaviour because we didn't want to receive her vocal wrath if we misbehaved.

When Tom and I got married, my brother Bill was one of our church ushers. Aunt Helen marched into the church and told Bill that she would sit beside Betty, her sister, in the front pew of the church. Bill tried to explain that that was reserved for Dad and the rest of Mom and Dad's family after Dad had given the bride away. No way was she going to stand for that. She was going to sit beside Betty and proceeded to seat herself down beside Betty despite Bill's quiet protests. I guess it all turned out okay because I wasn't there to referee. However, Bill was afraid to talk to her for quite a number of years. He felt she was still terribly mad at him for this incident, but I think she forgot it as soon as the wedding was over. That was Helen Carlson. She had a mind of her own, and everyone knew it.

Aunt Helen always had a great affection for the Italians because her home was right in the middle of the Italian community in Edmonton on

THREE WIEDEMAN SISTERS

96th street and 107th avenue. I think her affection stemmed from the fact that Italians seemed to be quite outspoken like she was, and she could understand them for this trait where others might be hurt by what she said even though she meant well. After Uncle Fred died, she became quite enamoured with an Italian man, Ugo, who lived with her for a number of years. When she was in ill health and needed to be confined to the General Hospital, he faithfully visited her every day. When she died, he looked after the disposal of her home and estate and immediately disappeared without any further communication with any members of Helen's family or any offer to let them have some of her precious keepsakes. I hope he is enjoying her money somewhere, I suspect, in Italy.

Uncle Bill - born March 23, 1917
Uncle Bill was the next child born to William and Mary in Myrtle, Manitoba. We never had the opportunity to meet Bill because he seemed to have an enormous amount of hostility towards most of the members of his family except for Suzanne, his closest sibling, whom he visited on occasion. Bill was, therefore, an enigma to us. We always thought he must have done something terribly wrong to ostracize himself from the family so completely. Some of us did try to reach him, but he always made it clear he didn't want anything to do with us. I thought that maybe because I was his niece and hadn't had anything to do with his previous life that maybe he wouldn't include me in his animosity. No such luck! He wrote, "Didn't I make it clear that I don't want anything to do with any of you?"

Bill's daughter, Sandra, visited us in the eighties to tell us the story of how she accidentally found out that she had twelve aunts and uncles that she didn't know existed. Her father had told her that he had no living relatives. When she was in Toronto at one point, she looked through the phone book to see if there were any Wiedemans listed there. She phoned a John Wiedeman and to her shock she discovered that John was her father's brother and her uncle. This was such a change of events in her life that she made the effort to visit as many of her Dad's relatives as possible, including two of his earlier children from Bill's first wife, Adeline, who lived in Camrose at the time. She didn't know anything about them either.

Without alerting her father, whom she knew would be quite angry over this discovery, Sandra contacted Aunt Susan and me in Edmonton. I was the oldest of all Grandma Wiedeman's grandchildren and was, at that time, working on the Family Tree. Susan and I had a wonderful visit, telling her as much as we knew about all of the Wiedeman family and history. At that time, Sandra was going with a Chinese fellow from Newfoundland, whom she eventually married, and I think she felt a kinship with my family because of our ethnic origins. Despite her resolve to keep her activities with her newfound relatives away from her dad, Sandra finally revealed to her father that she had contacted his family members unbeknownst to him. He was extremely angry, and she suffered his wrath for a while. Following Sandra's visit, we had visits from her brother, Paul, and some of Uncle Bill's first family members. It was good to finally get in touch with these folk that were such a mystery to the rest of us. Uncle Bill died a short time later, and I believe his whole family was relieved that Sandra had discovered the rest of us and had had a chance to talk about it with her dad even though he made no effort to reconcile with anyone.

Aunt Suzanne (Susan) – born November 14, 1918

Perhaps we knew Aunt Susan best of all Mom's family, excluding Nieta who was more of a sister to us than an aunt because I was almost her age. Susan was born in Myrtle, Manitoba, and seemed to know the history of those family days better than most of the others because she was in the middle of the clan and stayed at home longer than the older members who had to go to work sooner. Susan eventually went to Edmonton to live with Helen and her husband while she worked at various jobs, specifically Allis Chalmers, an implement dealership. When Grandma, Jake, and Nieta moved from Grande Prairie to Edmonton in 1951, Susan moved with them into a new home where she lived until her death.

When Betty moved to Edmonton after Dad died, she, Aunt Helen, and Aunt Susan were together quite a bit, especially to go grocery shopping because Susan had a car that the other two didn't. When Tom and I and our family was young, we hosted quite a few family gatherings and picnics. These three ladies always came together, and because they were all quite opinionated and sure of their ideas, they were not afraid to voice their arguments with gusto in our presence. Behind their backs we called them The Three Musketeers or sometimes the three amigos. Perhaps those terms are rather mild to describe their arguments with each other, but we never interfered because we knew they loved each other in their own ways and because

AUNT SUSAN AND GRANDMA IN FRONT OF THEIR BEAR CREEK HOME

they really needed each other. Betty, because she was the oldest, was given a certain kind of respect, but she always seemed to be at the centre of their comments. Betty had a varied background of independent ventures that the others didn't have. She had had a family of four lively children, a growing clan of grandchildren, was married to an entrepreneurial business man, and wasn't afraid to travel to various parts of the world to see her boys.

It always seemed to me that these vocal confrontations were tinged with a slight amount of jealousy or envy or one-upmanship on their parts depending on the topic argued. But in the end, they could all happily climb into Susan's car while she delivered each of them to their own abodes. On the way home, I am absolutely sure they argued about the right route to take.

Evelyn Marvin Millman

Aunt Susan, underneath her sometimes stern, inflexible exterior, was a most kind, considerate and generous woman. We had many happy dinners in her home with Grandma, Uncle Jake, and Nieta, and we were always the recipients of the produce from her garden, especially the zucchinis that never seemed to give up growing.

While Susan lived with Aunt Helen, she participated in the sewing bees the two of them had in making stuffed toys for us and the boxes of clothes they sent to Nieta in Grande Prairie twice a year. Susan never married, but her children were the nieces and nephews of her brothers and sisters whom she always welcomed with open arms if they happened to visit. At the time of Susan's death, there would have been twenty-seven living grandchildren of Grandma and Grandpa Wiedeman. If any of the Marvins were away for any length of time, we always made sure to pay a visit to her home when we came back.

UNCLE ED, AUNT HELEN, AUNT SUSAN

My earliest memories of Aunt Susan are of her hugging my little brother Billy when he was about two years old, chasing the little rascal around the house and calling him "my little McPherson." Now where on earth did she get the term "McPherson" unless it was the name of an old flame. We'll never know.

Aunt Olga - born March 13, 1920

AUNT OLGA WITH HUSBAND
RAY AND YOUNG FAMILY

I have a very faint recollection of Aunt Olga looking after us when we were small before she left to join the navy during World War II. She was born in Plum Coulee, Manitoba, and seemed to me to be the gentlest, most caring and soft spoken of all Grandma's girls with a happy laughter that made you feel comfortable with her immediately. Infrequently she brought her husband, Ray, and family of six children to Edmonton to visit Grandma and Susan from their home in California. Her girls were beautiful with their tanned complexions and long black hair, a result of the Mexican influence of their father. Cousin Suey, who lived in California, would visit them quite often and developed an affection for them all. I am sure her life was not easy with six kids to bring up and a husband who loved his bottle. She was, unfortunately, hit by a car while waiting to cross at an intersection and died immediately. It is to their credit that the family survived this tragic accident as best they could at a time in their lives when they needed their mother more than anything.

Grandma's next five children were all born in Plum Coulee, Manitoba, bringing to 12 the number that Grandma and Grandpa Wiedeman would bring to Alberta to live on the homestead their Dad was planning for them.

AUNT OLGA IN NAVAL UNIFORM

Uncle Henry – born December 10, 1921

Henry was a tall, slender, handsome man who also joined the navy during World War II with Alex and Olga. While stationed in Newfoundland, he met and married Audrey Payne. There he raised his family of four before moving to an acreage in Rockwood, Ontario. Uncle Henry was a fun-loving man who used to love giving his nieces the biggest bear hugs they had ever experienced when we visited. We were not used to that kind of affection. Henry had become a real Newfie. He loved the outdoors and took pride in building his own home on the acreage and having his children nearby so he could help them too. He worked for CN Railways and took the train each day to and from Rockwood to Toronto.

UNCLE HENRY IN NAVAL UNIFORM

HENRY'S WEDDING TO AUDREY

On one of our early visits to his acreage, on our way to a legal convention in Montreal, Tom and I stayed with them during the last game of a Canadian/Russian hockey series being played in Russia. At that time, Henry and Audrey's family all lived in a real old home on the acreage with Audrey's father because their new home was still just an idea. All of us were anxious to see this last game in the first series of hockey games that the Canadians and Russians had ever played against each other. After supper we all gathered around the small black and white screen to watch with anxious trepidation this game of the century. When the score looked like it was going to remain a tie at the end of the third period, the tension in the room was unbearable. Suddenly one of the Canadian players we had not heard of much, Paul Henderson, scrambled to get the puck and valiantly made his way towards the Russian net where he plunked it in to win the game amidst the absolute joy of everyone in the room—as well as everyone in Canada. We shall never forget that tense but wonderful evening with this fun-loving Newfie family of ours.

Uncle Henry and Audrey were of similar mindsets to that of Tom and me in that we always believed in creating memories by hosting family reunions or family celebrations of one kind or another whether it be a simple birthday dinner out for one of our children or a large gathering of friends and relatives to create a feeling of community at an anniversary celebration. Eventually Uncle Henry's new home got built with help from my brother Bill who drew up plans and drawings to guide them in its construction. There was always a room to stay in when we visited over the years.

Uncle John - born May 30, 1923

Uncle John and Uncle Henry seemed to follow each other to eastern Canada when they were looking for work before the War and had similar skills in construction and mechanical things. As was previously mentioned, they helped to renovate and enlarge Grandma's home in Grande Prairie so that it could more easily accommodate such a large brood. I shall never forget when a new sofa and easy chair from John arrived at Grandma's place to replace the blanket covered wood sofa that was initially used in the living room. Later he also sent a refrigerator to replace the ice box. These seemed to be such luxuries at that time. When my uncles joined the army and navy, my mother would have us children sit down at the dining room table and write letters to them that must have given them at least a few smiles when they read our juvenile musings at ages six and seven. These letters were always accompanied by boxes of cookies that Mom made to cheer them up. We had visions of them eating the cookies and reading our letters

UNCLE JOHN

UNCLE JOHN AND UNCLE ALEX
IN MILITARY UNIFORM

UNCLE JOHN
AND WIFE PEG

while waiting in the trenches during the war, but I don't think any of them were ever in trenches. Uncle John was a signaller in the army, and Henry and Alex were in navy transport ships.

Uncle John was always a favourite uncle of most of us. He was gentle and soft spoken and had an easy laugh and was always interested in what we were doing. After the war, he started a construction company that mainly renovated some of the wealthiest homes in the suburb of Rosedale in Toronto. Rosedale is one of the oldest suburbs in Toronto with some of the wealthiest families and the highest priced homes in Canada in its confines. Uncle John worked closely with Toronto's architects and designers to such an extent on these homes that he earned the nickname "Mr. Rosedale" although he did not live there. His workmanship was superb and he was well compensated. The several homes he designed and built for himself and his wife, Peg, were some of the most stylish homes I have been in. One particular duplex that he and his son Eric built on a narrow lot on one of the corners of Bay Street in the heart of the financial district was especially unique. It had three stories, a sunken garden and all the amenities of a thoroughly modern kitchen. John and Peg's son Eric lived in the other part of the duplex and it was even more modern in its layout. His main bathroom was one big room lined with ceramic tile from top to bottom with no stalls or dividing walls and with high placed windows all along one wall. For years it remained my dream bathroom.

When Uncle John retired, he sold this duplex and bought a large acreage several miles north of Toronto on which he and Peg planted the whole plot with lines of pine trees leaving enough space for him to build a new home and garden. This new home was more suited to the countryside but still contained all the luxuries of a city home. In a few years when the pines were grown, John and Peg made cross-country ski trails throughout this huge plot of land. When I was there one summer, walking under the pines on the thick layer of pine needles that had fallen in place over several years, it was like walking on a foot thick layer of foam or a foot thick layer of snow. It was difficult to walk in because every time you took a step you sunk into it rather than walking on the top of it. This wonderful home and land now belongs to the famous Canadian author Margaret Atwood where she can write in complete privacy away from city life.

Uncle John and Peg visited in Edmonton as often as possible. We always had so much fun when they were here, laughing at incidents in our earlier lives during hard times. We always agreed that the hard times were good for us because they taught us responsibility and hard work and gave us a good deal of self-esteem and self-worth.

Uncle Jacob (Jake) - born January 20, 1925

Mary and William's tenth child was Jacob or Jake as everyone called him. Uncle Jake contracted polio when he was about six months old, and a lot of his mother's decisions later were based on Jake's needs as he was quite severely crippled. He was a gentle young man with extreme determination that is sometimes evident in people with a physical disability. Each day when he went to school in Grande Prairie, he had to climb that hill in front of Grandma's home and then walk ten or so blocks to school and back. He did this every day of the twelve years of his school career in good weather and frigid weather, in deep snow or sloshing mud. There was no car or bus to drive him to and from school like there is for today's children.

He was a top student in school, and when he completed his high school diploma, he got his bookkeeping certification to prepare him for the job he secured at Joe Crummy's car dealership in Grande Prairie that was much closer to his home than was the school although he still had to climb the hill. When he earned enough money, he

UNCLE JAKE

bought an Austin Mini—a small English car suited to his frail stature. When he had to brake he lifted his leg with his hand and placed it on the brake pedal. As far as I know he never had a car accident in his eighteen years of driving.

While our other uncles were always too busy to bother much with us kids, Uncle Jake always had time to play Monopoly or Pick-up-sticks or Snakes and Ladders with us. In Monopoly he was always the banker so that kept us honest. Everyone respected him for his determination to be as normal as possible even though it took almost a superhuman effort to do the things he did. If anybody tried to help him, they would suffer his ability to swear at them in words we didn't hear very often. Several times I witnessed Uncle David or Uncle Ed, who were big strapping young men, lift him up and carry him up a flight of stairs while Jake kicked and hollered to no avail. To witness Jake's periodic epileptic seizures was a very frightening experience for us children who knew nothing about this kind of congenital ailment. Although these seizures usually left him quite weakened, he soon bounced back to his usual pleasant self and usually didn't even realize what he had just experienced.

For me and all of our family, it was a sad day in 1951 when Grandma, Uncle Jake, and Nieta all decided to move to Edmonton to buy a home there and live with Susan. Grandma sold her home for two hundred dollars, shipped their furniture and all their worldly goods to Edmonton, and packed the Austin to the rafters and left to drive the long road to Edmonton. I couldn't believe that they would forsake all of us who loved them so and the town that I thought had been so good for them. Jake found a job with the Canadian Army at Griesbach as a bookkeeper and Nieta at the Alberta Treasury Branch while Grandma settled into their new home with amenities like indoor plumbing that Grandma had never enjoyed in Grande Prairie or the homestead.

Uncle Ed – born March 18, 1926

UNCLE ED WITH HIS
SISTER AUNT HELEN

UNCLE ED IN HIS ARMY
UNIFORM IN ABOUT 1943

That left uncles Edward and David as the last of Grandma's sons at home. Uncle Ed joined the army during the war as a very young man and served as a security guard in a prison for German soldiers near Lethbridge for about two years before the war ended. These German prisoners were so impressed with how well they had been treated in Canadian POW camps that, after the war ended, many of them returned to live in Canada and to become Canadian citizens. Uncle Ed then went on to work in Slave Lake as a forest ranger for many years before going to Prince George in the same profession. On his many trips to Edmonton, he always came to visit us in our home in Parkallen. On one of his visits on the morning of November 22, 1963, he knocked on our door as I was busy tending to David and Margot who were about one and three years old. When I opened the door, he asked me if I had heard the news.

"No," I said. "I've been so busy with the kids. I haven't even had a chance to turn on the radio yet. What news?"

He then informed me that John F. Kennedy had just been assassinated. I thought maybe he was joking, but it wasn't much of a joke, so I immediately turned on the radio in the living room. At that stage we still didn't have a television set. So Ed and I listened to the sad news coming from Dallas, Texas, for the rest of the morning in absolute disbelief. Kennedy's presidency in the US seemed to usher in a new era of optimism and hope and youthfulness, and all the world was watching this young man to see if his inaugural address would bring change to a world still at war in many places. There are several moments in history that seemed to be seared into one's memory, and that day was one of them. I was glad Ed was there to announce this news and then to share the tragedy with me. Ed never married and died rather early in life, at age fifty-six, of a kind of cancer.

Uncle David - born September 14, 1927

Uncle David was always around with us whenever we visited Grandma in Grande Prairie although we were probably nothing but a big nuisance for him when he was a teenager and all four of us were much younger. Jack Jr. and Bill loved to see what interesting mechanical things the older uncles were experimenting with in their upstairs attic bedrooms—like early crystal radios. They had access to all the *Popular Mechanics* magazines the uncles bought, and I must say I found them most interesting too because they showed how to make all manner of furniture, mechanics and hobbies. I think that's where my two brothers got their appetite and flair for construction, engineering, architecture and all things mechani-

cal. Those weren't the only magazines our uncles bought, and I suspect that the cave they dug on the side of the hill with a padlocked door contained the other magazines that Grandma would have been shocked to let them have in their rooms.

UNCLE DAVID

As a young boy, David burned his leg badly in an accident involving gasoline and spent almost a year in the hospital with a tent-like structure over the stricken limb, waiting for the skin to grow back. But his leg continued to give him trouble for the rest of his life. In St. Albert, where David and his first wife Jean moved, he worked for a trucking company until later in his life when he could no longer continue working in such backbreaking labor. With Jean, David had two children, Rob and Deanna. Shortly after Rob married his wife, Debbie, Uncle David married Debbie's mother, Linda, which is a different turn of events in a family, but it has been nice for each of them to have found companionship with each other in their later years. David was always a very gentle, soft spoken man, whom we always included in our family reunions because he lived near us in Edmonton. Both Rob and David took an interest in my umbrella company later, and we appreciated their mechanical expertise on issues in which we could be quite ignorant. Both David and Linda were extremely good with our mother, Betty, taking her out for Chinese food when the rest of her children were too busy.

Aunt Nieta - born Jan.4, 1933

The last of Grandma's children, Nieta, was the only child born while the family lived on the Lymburn homestead. She became like a sister to us because she was only a little over a year older than me. In the early years, if she wasn't at our house, I was at her house. I often slept over between her and Grandma on a three quarters bed. The bed was so small for the three of us that I had to be as still as possible in order

AUNT NIETA IN HER HIGH
SCHOOL GRADUATION DRESS

NIETA AND HUSBAND BOB

not to disturb Grandma. Thankfully, at a young age, I slept so soundly that the coziness of it was not noticeable to me but I wonder now how Nieta and Grandma made out. They never complained, however, and I did it often so it must have been OK with them. Nieta and I were good friends and spent our spare time on Sundays wandering the hillsides around the Bear Creek Flats looking for the first Spring flowers or swinging on the neighbour's two seater wooden swing. Nieta was a real nature lover and a walker of the highest order—so different from me, but I tagged along. Nieta was one year ahead of me in school, and when she was in grade seven in junior high, she insisted that I call her Aunt Nieta. I refused to do it because we really didn't use those terms for any of our older aunts and uncles. We just used their names, but I am not sure why. It seemed to be the custom, and our parents never insisted otherwise. For about a year she was more than a little peeved with me but soon we both got over it and were good friends again.

Nieta later married Robert (Bob) Duff in Vancouver, and they had two children, Malcolm and Kathryn. Unbeknownst to Nieta, brother Jack had previously met Bob when he went to the University of Manitoba in Winnipeg. They had both stayed in the same residence, and both were pursuing their respective engineering degrees there. One day, Jack dropped in for a surprise visit to see Nieta who was living in Vancouver at the time going to University there. It so happened that Bob had also stopped in for a visit when he was courting Nieta. He was completing his final electrical engineering degree at the University of British Columbia.

"What are you doing here with my aunt?" asked a very surprised Jack who never expected such a chance encounter with a friend from his university days.

With all of Grandma's thirteen children settled in Grande Prairie or nearby, you can probably sense that either our dad would be extremely excited to all of a sudden have inherited Mom's siblings, or else be fearful that such a large gang would impose on him in some way. And you can see how all these aunts and uncles of ours would find all these four adorable little urchins nice to coddle and spoil so long as they didn't have to be responsible for them. We were some of Grandma's first grandchildren and the first nieces and nephews. You can also understand that we must have also been a big nuisance for them at times. In actual fact they were wonderful to us. They babysat when Mom needed some respite. They put up with little children at the dinner table. They played games with us. And we wrote letters to them, visited with them in various places as we became adults, invited them to our homes for family gatherings or for picnics, and generally considered them part of a well-loved extended family. Each of them was so different, but they all had inherited those traits of their forefathers that made them skillful with their hands, industrious and hard working.

For my birthdays, Grandma would always make homemade chicken noodle soup with *homemade* noodles, my favourite German dish. And Nieta would give me a jar of green pickled olives stuffed with pimento. This definitely was a rarity for me. I would put the jar in my bedroom drawer to hide it from the others and take one olive a day, roll it around in my mouth for a while and then savour it ever so privately. Oh my goodness, it tasted *so* good! Now I prefer the black olives.

Birthdays in those harsh economic times for us were never big celebrations as they are for today's children. In all our years, we never had a birthday party or a birthday cake. Simple pleasures like chicken soup or a jar of olives were special enough.

CHAPTER ELEVEN

Chinese Family and Friends

The Lee Taks

Until about 1945 we were the only children of a mixed Chinese parentage in the whole of the Peace River Country. In Spirit River, Mr. Lee Tak worked in the local hotel, and his wife ran a beauty parlour in their tiny home. Both were of Chinese ethnicity and they had three children named June, David and Laddie. Mom and Dad sent me to their home every summer for two weeks in the hope that I would become more acclimatized to the Chinese culture and perhaps learn the Cantonese dialect—something I never did. It was difficult to do this in our home with the two different first languages of my parents, for they had to speak English to understand each other. The Lee Tak family adopted me as their surrogate child while in their care and gave me a Chinese name. I loved being the youngest in the family instead of the oldest.

This was in the era of Shirley Temple, the famous child actress of

MRS. LEE TAK AND EVELYN

the late thirties and early forties. Since Mrs. Tak was a hairdresser, she took the opportunity to give my straight black hair a 'curls all over your head' Shirley Temple look. I hated it, but I hated the curling irons hooked up to a central heating mechanism even more. I had to sit for about an hour with about thirty hot curling irons hooked up to my small head. It felt like I was being held captive as a prisoner and there was no way to get up or run away without losing my scalp to the hot curlers. Otherwise, my visits to the Lee Taks were special.

Spirit River is situated about fifty miles north of Grande Prairie on a long rolling hill overlooking the prairie, grain fields, and forests on all sides. You can see for miles around. David, who was the youngest in the family, would perch me on the crossbar of his bicycle and drive me all around Spirit River and all over that hill. Was he trying to get out of doing his chores, or was he bored with life in the small town? I was too young to know that.

The Lee Taks were special friends of my mother too. At least they spoke good English, so Mom could communicate easily with these most friendly of our Chinese friends. When they moved to Edmonton to open up a small grocery store on 95th Street and 106th Avenue, we would visit them every year when we came to the city. Mrs. Tak opened her hair salon on the second floor above the store, but I was afraid to patronize her for fear she would do something to my hair that I wouldn't like with memories of my youth when they lived in Spirit River. Their small family home in the city was at the back of their store. Their oldest daughter, June, was much older than me, but because she played the piano, we had a common interest and would often play piano duets together. When she left for Vancouver to get married, the Lee Taks persuaded me to take her place playing the small electric organ at the Chinese United Church on 96th Street when I was in my first year of University. I would play the hymns and musical interludes, but sitting through an hour or more of language I couldn't follow was a bit much for me. So after the year was over, I didn't go back.

Mrs. Tak, being the proverbial Chinese matriarchal matchmaker, tried her best to find a Chinese boyfriend for me, but I didn't appreciate that much. So after the first unsuccessful date with a Chinese engineering student, I made it quite clear that I could find my own dates. I didn't want to hurt her feelings, but I also had my own life to lead and it wasn't the old fashioned Chinese way.

The Yules

During World War II another mixed race Chinese-English family moved to Grande Prairie for a brief period. Mr. Yule was in the army and had brought his English bride to Canada from Great Britain. They had three school-aged children named Lily, Leona and Albert. The girls were a few years older than us Marvins and caused quite a stir in our high school because they were so beautiful. The high school boys quickly fell in love with them. Albert was in brother Jack's class. Mom befriended Mrs. Yule as was her usual custom. Eventually they all moved to Edmonton after the war was over, and we lost track of them. I am not sure what Mr. Yule's participation in the army was, but I suspect that, because he was an older man and had come from England, that perhaps he was in Canada in some educational capacity for the Canadian Army battalion that was then stationed in our town.

SOME OF THE YULE FAMILY

Evelyn Marvin Millman

Leong Chong

When we were growing up, there were two shoemakers on the main street; one was German, and the other was Chinese. The one my mother sent us to was a Chinese immigrant, like my father, named Leong Chong.

His little shop was an afterthought, like a lean-to, built between two other big brick buildings on our main street, now called Richmond Avenue. It was one long room no wider than eight feet and the full length of the other two buildings. It contained all his meagre earthly goods for living and working. His shoe repair equipment was near the front window with a cot and a few other kitchen supplies in the back. The only light was from the front window and a small light on his shoe anvil.

Leong Chong loved children, and when you went into his shop, you had to stay and socialize with him for a while before he would let you go. His English was limited, but we could understand him because he was so genuine in his love for children. The photo of my three siblings and I, given to him by my dad and taken by the local photographer, hung on his wall near the front door for everyone to see when they came to have their shoes repaired. It was almost like he had adopted us through that photo to remind him of what it would have been like to have had his family with him there. We became his surrogate children every time we came to see him. I hope that we returned that love when we walked in the door of his shop. I am not sure about others who visited his shop, but he never charged us for any of the repairs on our shoes. Instead he always had a small store of candy to dispense to us when we left.

I can still picture Leong Chong in my mind when we brought in the loose soles of our shoes that flapped around when we ran to school. While we sat in the chair and waited, he would put our shoe on the anvil, some little nails in his mouth, and proceed to glue the sole back on, take out the nails in his mouth one at a time, pound them in with his hammer, and, voila! our shoes were ready to put back on.

About thirty years ago, my sister, Eva, travelled back to Grande Prairie with my son Peter to visit the town, which had become a city, and to see the changes that had occurred since she left to pursue her nursing career in various parts of the world before settling in Calgary. She went to the old shoe repair shop that had been taken over by someone else. To her surprise, there on the wall by the front door, in exactly the same spot it had been before, was the photo of all of us children.

"Do you know who those children are?" she asked the shopkeeper.

"No, I haven't a clue. I've just left the photo there because I have more important work to do than decorate this lowly shoe repair shop," said the owner.

"I'd love to have it, if it's not important to you. Those four children are my brothers and sister and I when we were very young. We were born and raised here in Grande Prairie. In the fifties and sixties we left to pursue our educations elsewhere. Now we are all over Alberta, and for some, in other parts of the world too," said Eva. "We used to bring our shoe repairs to this shop to Leong Chong who loved children and became a trusted friend of ours whenever we entered his shop."

"You are welcome to take it," said the owner. "I am glad to find someone who wants it."

So Eva carefully took the photo off the wall to treasure in her book of photos.

During the early part of the twentieth century, the Chinese in our town, without exception, were single men without their families. After their hard work in the restaurants, the laundries, or shoe repair shop, time was long on their hands and loneliness was a constant companion. Gambling, especially Mah Jong, became a major past time. Getting together for their evening meals in the Chinese tradition, in one or another of the Chinese restaurants' back kitchens, kept them in touch with each other to reminisce about the homeland, to talk about the Japanese War and invasion on Chinese territory, and to help each other to understand the Canadian way, with its myriad laws and regulations in a new land so different from theirs. Even though most of their conversations would be in the Cantonese Chinese dialect, an important part of socializing with their fellow countrymen would be to get help in English language usage.

Evelyn Marvin Millman

Leong Chong seemed to gravitate to the Chinese men in the Royal Café who were mostly Wongs, and I presume that's where he would go for his evening meal and from whom he would get his social support. Now, when my memories take me back to my childhood, I often think about that old friendly stooped-over Chinese man who took such an interest in our family. What brought him to Canada, and what hardships did he endure when he found himself in this land so different from his own? Did he think he was coming to the land of the Golden Mountain to make a fortune? Did he have a wife and children back in China that he would never see because his small salary certainly could not have supported that luxury? Did he send money back as so many Chinese immigrants were expected to do to support their family back home? Was his family killed during the Japanese invasion as so many were? Did he get homesick? Who looked after him when he was old and sick? Was anyone there when he died?

Now that I have had the privilege of visiting Leong Chong's homeland several times, I wish that I could have also had the opportunity to travel back to Grande Prairie to talk to him about what I was for-tunate to experience and witness in a vastly changed land from what he knew in his youth. It is so sad that, in my childhood, I didn't have the maturity and interest to spend more time with him and to ask more questions about his life. However, it has given me a great source of comfort to know that someone cared enough about him to erect a grave and headstone in the Grande Prairie Cemetery.

LEONG CHONG'S GRAVESTONE

Restaurant Travels in the Peace

As young children, our memories in the summer months included visiting practically every Chinese restaurant in the Peace River Country with our mom and dad. Ou travels took us to Peace River, Valleyview,

High Prairie, Athabasca, Fairview, Spirit River, Dawson Creek, and McLennan, to name a few. I remember Dad would come home and tell Mom,

"Get the kids ready. We're going to Peace River."

Mom would have us ready in half an hour or less. We didn't pack suitcases or toothbrushes. We just wore the clothes we had on and jumped in the car and off we would go for an exciting day or more. While Dad held court in the back kitchens of all the Chinese restaurants we passed along the way, Mom would watch over us kids as we roamed the new terrain or patiently waited for Dad to finish his visiting.

For Dad it was actually *more* than visiting; it was a chance for him to help his compatriots if they had any problems. He had access to advice in Grande Prairie from the business friends who patronized his restaurant. However, it was most important for him to keep in touch with his countrymen wherever they might be. The patience of our mother was amazing, but she enjoyed the car ride and getting away from her daily routine. She, and all of us, cherished the meals and generosity we experienced from these welcoming people along Alberta's roads and towns. As youngsters, we were privileged to see more of our country with our visits along the way to Kelowna and Edmonton and spots in the Peace River Country than most of our peers and friends. We ate in all the Chinese restaurants along the way and saw some of the most unique scenery available in Alberta and British Columbia.

How privileged we were as young spirited rascals. We had a very proud father of whom we also were so proud because he became the most Canadian of all the Chinese men we knew during our youth, and because he was so well respected by the Chinese friends we met. And we had an extremely patient mother who loved the travels then as she did later in life when we were all gone from home and Dad had died. When Mom wasn't sitting on orange crates and apple boxes in the back kitchens of these little restaurants, she was watching over us as we explored another new town along the way.

CHAPTER TWELVE

Chinese Cuisine in the 1940s and Beyond

Recently at the Royal Alberta Provincial Museum in Edmonton featured a display called "Chop Suey on the Prairies." I hope that the creators of this display did not mean to imply that Chinese food was not offered to customers other than in Edmonton, Calgary, and Lethbridge—the larger cities in the province—until after the forties. That was what many, who ought to have known better, took away from that display unfortunately. Those of us of Asian ethnic origin who grew up in small towns and villages of Alberta know that Chinese cuisine was indeed on the menus of their cafés and was served to many who were willing to adventure into a new and tasty cuisine. Unfortunately, not enough research had been done on this topic, and patrons of the museum were left with the wrong message. The creator of that display should maybe have concentrated on doing some research in smaller centres rather than just in the bigger cities. This museum display has prompted the inclusion of this chapter, for we were fortunate in our youth to be exposed not only to Chinese food but also to our Grandmother's German cuisine which really became the major fare in our home and in that of most of my friends. It seemed to us to be Canadian.

In our childhood travels with Mom and Dad, most of the little restaurants in the small towns we visited offered Chinese food in their menus, and in some places it was the only thing we could order. Western food was offered too because, otherwise, they would not have attracted a more widespread western clientele. Chinese food, however, was gradually becoming a popular cuisine. After high school, my brother Jack worked in the Peacock Inn in Red Deer where it was served to local food aficionados in that town during the fifties. With many Canadians, as in the older members of my mother's family, at first Chinese cuisine was suspicious. Their major concern was about cleanliness and their unfamiliarity with the different exotic ingredients used. Our Dad was quite meticulous about cleanliness, and his restaurant was closed for two weeks every February so that it could be thoroughly washed, painted and cleaned in every corner. If there was food like bread or meat that needed to be used up before the painters came, Dad brought it home to Mom where she welcomed it to feed her hungry clan. This closure also gave an opportunity for the Chinese staff to go back to China to visit their families.

The Lingnan Restaurant
On our visits to Edmonton in the late forties, the first thing our family did upon arrival, whether it was 9 pm or 2 am, was to visit the Lingnan Restaurant, which was at that time on 97th street on the second floor just off Jasper Avenue. Our dad was a good friend of the proprietor there, Mr. Philip Pon. So the first thing they did together was to enjoy a Chinese feast and then a game of golf the next day. Chinese food was offered there on the menu in the forties, fifties and sixties. It was easier to get all the special ingredients needed for Chinese food in the city than it was in Grande Prairie. Later in our visit, we would invite my mother's German relatives to join us for dinners where they also became more intimately acquainted with the cuisine offered. However, other than Nieta, they never developed the same fondness for Chinese cuisine that we had. And I recall my Aunt Susan, who I was sitting beside at one meal, leaning over and saying to me, "My dear, you smell very garlicky," which led me to be quite

concerned about my breath. We know now that garlic is very good for you, but if you don't want to have bad breath, don't eat it raw. The secret to the wonderful aromas of Chinese food is the combination of garlic and ginger as well as the addition of all the variable sauces that we have access to now—oyster, black bean, hoisin, Szechwan, soy sauce and five spice powder to name a few.

My Aunt Helen and her husband, Fred, lived at 9650 - 107th Avenue, just three houses east off 97th St. Today it is the site of the Lucky 97 Safeway Store. It was so safe in the city at that time that our parents and Aunt Helen would let us kids go on our own along 97th Street to see Dad who was visiting Philip Pon at the Lingnan. Sometimes we would stop to visit Aunt Susan too. At that time she worked at a Lebanese grocery store on the same street right beside the underpass for the train tracks on 104th Avenue. When we reached the Lingnan, Dad loved to show us all off to Philip Pon and his wife who were never able to have children of their own although they adopted a daughter, Valeen, who became a journalist specializing in travel destinations.

ROM RIGHT TO LEFT: PHILIP PON, MRS. PON, DAD, EVELYN, EVA, UNKNOWN, MOM, UNKNOWN

As I mentioned earlier, it is a very real possibility that both Dad and Philip may have worked as house boys in the famed Rogers "Sugar Shack" home in Vancouver when they first arrived in Canada. Dad never mentioned the exact place where he worked as a houseboy, but he and Philip had so much to talk about when they got together that it seems a distinct possibility. They always spoke in their Chinese dialect, so we never knew what they were talking about.

During my university years, when Mom and Dad came to Edmonton, they would always invite the friends with whom I lived to join all of us in our Chinese repast at the Lingnan even if it was after midnight.

Early in my marriage with Tom, Dad phoned one night about 2 am.

"Mom and I just got into Edmonton. We're here at the Lingnan. Why don't you and Tom join us for a meal."

I was game because I loved eating out, especially Chinese food, and because I was so used to this behaviour of my Dad. Tom was a little less sure.

"At this time of night? You've got to be kidding. I have clients to see early in the morning."

So I happily went by myself, even though I, too, had a job at the university to go to in the morning. It was a good opportunity for me to see and visit with my parents on these few occasions and to appreciate their late night hospitality.

The Palace Restaurant Life

As I mentioned earlier, Dad was a bit of a mystery to us children because he didn't participate in our daily family life except when we were on holidays. He was always there in the morning when we awoke but left early for the restaurant where we assumed he made his breakfast and got things started for the day. The few times we had his pancakes at the restaurant they were simply delicious. I often watched him make them when I had to go and ask him for money for something at school. They were made directly on the big restaurant stovetop that was basically one huge cast iron griddle with wood or coal fires underneath fed from the front of the open stove rather than the top like our stove at home with its stove lids. The batter was in a large pot or tin can with a ladle that looked like it was made out of string. He would lift the ladle out of the batter over the greased stove until there was enough batter for the pancake dripping from the string ladle. The pancakes were flipped and turned out to perfection. In town, Dad became renowned for his pancake batter, and the perfect pancakes that attracted the town bachelors and anyone in need of a good breakfast. Those were the days before Smitty's, Denny's, Albert's, IHOP and other famous eateries snow specializing in pancakes. His batter, as well as his coffee, were secrets in those days and remain so to this day.

Cooking Lessons

Except for the few times that Dad taught Eva and I how to make perfect jelly rolls and macaroons, we never had the opportunity to learn his culinary skills. Everything we did was by hand without the cooking tools that fill the kitchen and gourmet stores in our present age. There were no mix masters, food processors, blenders or wand mixers. I would mix the sugar and butter together for what seemed hours with a large spoon and finally ask Dad if it was enough. He would take a twirl with the spoon and shake his head.

"You can still feel the grains of the sugar. You have to stir it until the batter is perfectly smooth and you cannot hear or feel the grains against the bowl when you are stirring."

So a-stirring we would go again until we finally got the right consistency. We never made those treats very often until we had the opportunity later in life to have better cooking gadgets. We certainly never forgot those few cooking lessons though.

In the restaurant, Dad was the one who taught his employees their skills whether it be in the kitchen or with the patrons. Mostly he was in the front end of the restaurant, greeting his customers, making sure the waitresses did their jobs, operating the cash register and, in between these times, doing the bookkeeping with the help of his Chinese abacus. He loved the opportunity to get to know the important town fathers who regularly met to drink coffee around the big oak table near the front entrance and close to the spittoon—an important fixture at that time in most cafés.

Dad's Coffee

The coffee that Dad made himself responsible for was another unique feature of his restaurant. Mom made the muslin coffee liners for the big coffee urn, and when Dad put the coffee grounds in the urn he also put in an egg or two mixing it together with the grounds to coagulate them together. This made the coffee come out perfectly clear and mellow. I loved to go grocery shopping with Mom on Saturday afternoons, stopping at the restaurant, and savouring the delicious coffee brew that Dad made for us before our walk home. Maybe it was my youth, or the fact that it was a new taste for me at the time—or my present memory loss—but I have really never had the same coffee taste experience since.

CHAPTER THIRTEEN

Life with Dad

Dad, like most of us, was not a perfect person although we all had an enormous respect and awe of him. His major fault was that, even though he was married, he really remained a bachelor for most of his life although he enjoyed the idea of having a wife and family he could boast about. He loved his children and, like most fathers, played with us in our early years whenever he had his afternoons off. If we heard him coming home, we would hide behind the door or wall and jump out to frighten him, and he in turn would fake being scared.

Like many fathers of his day, his occupation took up most of his day, leaving him little room to do that great a job of mentoring his children in the sense of being a friend that one could talk to about your problems. He made sure we knew what he expected of us, but it was up to Mom to do the disciplining and nurturing. He knew that his kids were a very visible minority of mixed ethnic cultures that sometimes aroused suspicion and curiosity by the prevailing European citizens of the town. He often said things like:

"I want Jack Marvin's kids to be good students and well behaved citizens. I want you to make something of yourself."

How we were to do that was not going to make a hole in his finances though. Looking back on Dad's history with us, it appears to me that he was not a very good money manager. At least Mom or us kids were never the receivers of it. However, money while we were young didn't seem to be a big issue like it did when we grew older. If Dad had money, he spent it generously, if he didn't have it, he didn't spend it and that was that. Somehow we always had plenty to eat, a roof over our heads, and no worries.

Jack's Restaurant Partners

If Dad was a mystery to us, so too was the restaurant. Who exactly owned it? Dad had several partners, and we just assumed they were the various Mahs that were involved in the restaurant. We children had a nickname for each of them, and each of them had a specific duty in the restaurant.

Mah Yin (Sam's father), did most of the cooking and the meat cutting. Carcasses of beef and pork hung on hooks in a big walk-in refrigerator, and he would cut them up on a huge wooden chopping table similar to the ones in butcher shops. He also made the long strings of sausages. He was a jolly soul who loved to tease us, but he always had a cleaver in his hand, so we didn't get too close, at least when we were little. We called him 'the fat cook' because he was a good size.

Mah Bing, who was the youngest of all the men, did a little bit of everything, but not much of anything, or so it seemed to us. We didn't have much to do with him, but when his daughter came to Grande Prairie in 1949, I was her bridesmaid at her arranged marriage to a Chinese fellow from Texas.

Mah Tah was Dad's first cousin, and we called him *Tah Soak* meaning [uncle]. He was the pastry chef who made the cakes, pies and anything sweet. He was a favourite but very shy. We called him 'the slim cook' because of his build. When Mah Tah was able to bring his wife and son Don to Canada in 1949, my mother gave Dad's Chinese Bible to Mah Tah's wife. Mah Tah was was about fifteen years younger than Dad and became his most intimate relationship of all his partners. As I mentioned previously, Dad's father (our grandfather in China) and Mah Tah's father were brothers.

Mah Hee was short with a huge stomach. Behind his back we simply called him *fat*. He seemed to hover around the cash register when Dad wasn't around, so I guess he had some idea of how to make change. Mah Hee had a small elegant home with lots of silk pictures on the wall and nice furniture. He married a native girl, and there were many wild parties at his house. At one of the parties he was thrown down the stairs and died, leaving a very young son fatherless. We never found out what happened after that.

Charlie Mah was a late comer to the restaurant, and we could never figure out why he was there. He also was in charge of the till after Mah Hee's tragic death. Our mother never liked Charlie Mah, and from her few comments it seemed like he had ulterior motives for being in the restaurant. He was a pretty good gambler, but had he gotten a share of the restaurant through his gambling as we suspected? According to Sam, our Dad never gambled, so it must have been one of the other men who might have gotten in too deep since they were known to play Mah Jong into the wee hours of the morning after the restaurant closed. In Dad's later years, he just left the Palace Café and went over to the Donald Café where he had other compatriots to be their front end man. We never questioned this move, but I think Dad just got disgusted with so many shareholders with their hands in the till and walked away. He didn't need that in his senior years and neither did Mom.

The restaurant continued to be a part of the dining culture of Grande Prairie, especially with younger men, but was eventually sold and removed for another building to be constructed on that site. Our closest link to the Palace Restaurant scene in the new city of Grande Prairie was Sam Mah, a distant cousin who came to Grande Prairie after 1949 by his father, Mah Yin, when the Government of Canada opened the immigration doors for the families of the Chinese single men in our country.

Teaching English to the Young Chinese Boys
One summer evening shortly after Sam Mah's arrival, Dad brought him and three other Chinese lads to our home. He decreed that each of us four children were to attempt to teach them English. None of them could speak or understand it. So I got Sam Mah, Jack got Mah

SAM AND WIFE

Bing's son, Eva got Suey Ning, and I have forgotten who Bill got. With the exception of Suey Ning, each of these boys was the son of someone in the restaurant. We noticed that Suey Ning did the hardest work in the restaurant and that his hands were swollen and rough from washing dishes and being in water for long periods of time. In those days, there was no such thing as an automatic dishwasher like there is in our modern restaurant kitchens. It was all done by hand, and when you are doing this all day long, it can leave your hands in quite rough shape. We all felt sorry for Suey Ning and felt there was something different about him—but what was it? He was very friendly and smiled a lot but didn't last long with us. We learned later from Dad that he was the "paper son" of Mah Bing and was here illegally taking the place of a son who died in China. Mah Bing brought him to Canada, requiring Suey to work for nothing for two years in the restaurant. I have no idea if there was any further remuneration that Suey had to pay, but I am quite sure this certainly did not meet the approval of Dad and might have been one of the reasons he did not stay with the Palace Café for long after that. Several years later, we read in the Vancouver newspaper that Suey had married and brought a wife back to Canada. It was newsworthy because, when she finally arrived in Canada, she declared that she was not going to be his wife and left for who knows where. It was a big story not only in the newspaper but local radio as well.

Sam Mah, who became my student, was a keen learner whom I felt had the potential to get his senior matriculation. I encouraged him to contact Mr. Walter Kujath, the principal of the Grande Prairie High School, and Mr. Harold McNeil, the social studies teacher, to discuss the possibility of becoming a mature student and furthering his education with supervision. I was on my way to university in Edmonton, so I was not able to encourage him to follow up on this plan. He did this entirely on his own, making his family later in his life immensely proud of their dad. Sam always had the deepest respect and reverence for my father and regarded him as a mentor in his life when he came to Canada. So at the weddings of Sam's children, I was given the opportunity to speak to the family and the assembled guests about what both Sam and my dad had done as new Canadian immigrants to become respected citizens of their new country.

CHAPTER FOURTEEN

World War II (1939-46)

Military Army Convoys

When World War II began, life became quite exciting in our town for us children. Army convoys began to come through the centre of Grande Prairie right past our small white cottage, located on Clairmont Road two short blocks from Dad's restaurant on the main street—now Richmond Avenue. There were hundreds of army trucks carrying thousands of khaki-clad young boy soldiers—many of them Afro-Americans. Clairmont Road was the main artery into Grande

Prairie in those days, and often the trucks would stop right in front of our home for long periods of time either to rest or to stock up on what the town had to offer like water and toilets and meals. During those times we four Marvin kids would straddle the white picket fence surrounding our home to watch the unending parade of vehicles go by and to chat with the soldiers, who were very friendly, whenever they stopped.

For one of her birthdays, Eva had just received a small grey baby kitten

EVA WITH KITTEN

as a pet. I remember her hugging it to her chest while she watched the proceedings.

As time wore on, the kitten learned to escape her clutches, and the soldiers began to play with it. They begged Eva to let them take the kitten with them, at which time our Mom had to intervene to see if Eva was agreeable to this. Mom explained to Eva that the men were so far away from home that they sometimes got homesick. The kitten would be a great pet for them when they were on the road and would keep them from feeling sad. Eva finally regretfully agreed after getting assurances that they would take good care of it—and that she could get another one soon.

Other times, when the troops came through the town early in the mornings, they would wake our parents to request that they would like them to make a good breakfast for them at the restaurant. At my young age, I would be pressed into babysitting my brothers and sister, and off would go my mother and father for most of the morning. We would mostly stay sleeping, but as I ponder this state of affairs, I wonder at the wisdom of it. Today this would not be tolerated before a concerned neighbour would phone 911 or the police to report child abuse or children left home alone. It would certainly draw some legal concerns, but in the forties in a small town this was often normal with many families, and indeed it made us grow up quickly with responsibilities at a much younger age than is usual today.

I suspect that the soldiers were on their way to build the Alaska Highway, since this project was a high priority for both the Canadian and American governments. Its importance was to create a land linkage between mainland US and Alaska through Canada. It would also provide a means to send supplies overland to the west coast in the event the Japanese war escalated to our shores. Canada was opposed to this highway construction project but finally relented on the condition that the US finance its building and hand it back to Canada when it was completed, which was done. The project strung a highway from Dawson Creek, British Columbia, to Delta Junction, Alaska, a distance of over 2,700 km and was miraculously completed in one year in (1942) when I was eight years old. Thousands of US soldiers were pressed into its building in unfamiliar and difficult muskeg and gumbo terrain, extreme frigid weather, sometimes hostile natives and other circumstances that they were not used to. Most of the soldiers lived in the southern states, so these northern conditions were totally foreign to them. The fiftieth anniversary of the completion of the Alaska Highway was commemorated in 1992. The highway has been greatly improved since 1942, and is now completely paved. It has proven to be beneficial for Canada in helping to open parts of northern Canada and in providing a major transit link from the far north to the far south.

Our First Home

The first home that I can remember was that small white bungalow with a kitchen, living room, two small bedrooms and a dugout basement that housed a coal furnace, coal bin, shelves for canned goods and an indoor portable toilet. While Mom and Dad had a nice high bed, we children slept on two metal springs and mattresses, each spring sitting on four big blocks of tree stumps. We had to be careful that we didn't move around much or else the metal spring would fall off the block on one corner and chaos would ensue. There was so little space in our small bedroom with two so-called beds, a small crib (when Bill was a baby) and a standalone closet. The living room had hardwood floors with scatter rugs. We would pretend that each rug was a boat, and we'd slide the rugs around on the highly waxed floors visiting each other on our rug boats. What imaginations! There was a Heintzman upright piano for the singsongs with lots of oriental framed silk pictures on the walls. The bookstand housing twenty volumes of the *Books of Knowledge* was a treasure. We would pore over its contents, art works, crafts and stories with intense interest because we had no other books. The town didn't have a library until later, and I cannot remember that there ever was a bookstore while I lived there.

The southwest corner of the house had a small patio with slat fencing that was about eight feet high and completely covered with hops and prickly inedible fruit in summer. It was a great place for all of us children to bathe and splash in the tub of water in privacy during the few hot summer days we had.

DAD WITH FOUR MARVIN URCHINS

The yard was fairly large surrounded by a white picket fence and large poplar trees so typical of the prairie landscape. As we got old enough to walk the top rail of the fence without falling, those of us who were able each took ownership of a poplar for a treehouse, traversing the top of the fence and visiting each other on the huge branches. Under the poplar trees, ran a sidewalk for residents of the street. I would like to say that we kept very quiet as people walked by on their way to shop for groceries or to pick up their mail occasionally looking up to offer their hellos. The most intriguing sight for us four urchins was when the local nuns from the Catholic Church nearby walked by in groups of two or four on their way to the post office or who knows where. In those days, they were dressed totally in long black habits with starched white surpluses that covered their heads and shoulders. We were deathly silent and awed as they walked by below us in our trees.

In those days, girls mostly wore dresses, and many times when we jumped down from the top of the fence, our skirt would get caught on one of the pickets and we either had to call for help while we hung there or wriggle as our skirt ripped to let us loose. Oh what fun we had without any toys or technical instruments! Oh what a lot of work for our mother to mend our clothes after the fence climbing! However, Mom must have enjoyed the brief respite from indoor sibling squabbles in order to do her ironing or baking without interruption.

At the far end of the fence, on the outside of one corner, was an icehouse filled with huge blocks of ice taken from the Wapiti River during winter when the river was frozen several feet deep. The ice was buried in sawdust to insulate it from the heat. The big door to it was left open during summer, and when the heat of the day got too unbearable, we would walk along the top of the fence to the icehouse and play in the sawdust. There were no refrigerators as we know them today, but many folks might have had an icebox to keep food like milk and butter or meat cold. People would put ice in the top compartment of the icebox, but it would have to be replaced every few days after the ice melted and lost its coldness. Because the ice was from the river, it was not used for drinking.

Within the perimeter of the fence, our dad planted a garden in the summer during his time off from the restaurant. Sweet peas grew along a wire fence that divided the plot into two parts, peonies and bleeding hearts in the front yard and vegetables elsewhere. Quite near the house were small cold frames for starting spring bedding plants of flowers as well as vegetables like cabbage, cauliflower, tomatoes and things like herbs. Both Mom and Dad led a busy life tending and watering this necessary hobby. Dad was a perfectionist when it came to starting and growing his plants, and eventually this hobby expanded to a farm he rented on the outside of town.

Late Night Singsongs
In that first little home of ours, I would often wake up at night to hear men lustily singing in our living room after midnight. The restaurant closed late at night with some of the itinerant salesmen still hovering

around with nothing else to do. Perhaps they had travelled all day to finally get to Grande Prairie or they had been visiting in other small centres during a week away from the big city of Edmonton. Dad would invite them home, especially if they were interested in singing. Dad could only play with one finger, so if someone else could play the piano, they went to it with great gusto with Mom and the rest of us sleeping away as best we could in our tiny house. I cannot recall that these musical moments caused me any sleeping problems, and I sometimes would sneak out of bed to watch these adult men enjoy their singing sessions so enthusiastically—my Dad most of all. He had most of the sheet music that was currently popular in that day, and he was happiest in his life when he could show off his exceptional voice to others.

Those late night singalongs were quite a regular occurrence in our home, and they became a pattern that eventually spread to us kids when we were in our teens. Dad loved for us to bring our friends home for an evening of hymn singing so he could join us and again show off his beautiful voice. He would even close the restaurant early to accommodate our earlier hours. My friends' love of this was greatly increased by the treats Dad brought. Actually they loved it more than his children did as we tried to overcome our initial embarrassment over such an enthusiastic singing Dad. Even without our friends there, Dad would often wake me up when he came home and say, "Evelyn, let's do some singing." So with me at the piano, we would go to it for an hour or so in between sips of tea while the rest of the family slept.

Cattle Drives

There was another exciting event that occurred twice a year and captivated small children while we lived in that little white house on Clairmont Road. Billy Salmond had a ranch north of the town some-where along the Clairmont Road where he raised his herd of cows and horses. In the early spring, he and his ranch hands would herd the cattle through town along the road in front of our home to some place south of the town where there was greener pasture. No way did we want to miss this exciting event, and up on the picket fence we would perch as the hundreds of mooing cows passed us by while the ranch hands and dogs tried their best to keep the cattle in line. Then in the autumn, they would do the same thing only this time the cows were being herded back to the ranch to their winter home, and we again watched with glee from our fence perches. What excitement for little kids!

Our Second Home

When our small white bungalow got too small for four growing children, my mother tried to get Dad interested in finding another home that was bigger. He was either too busy at the restaurant or didn't want to leave the yard where he had experimented with growing vegetables for the restaurant in a cold climate he wasn't familiar with. Everything was exceptionally well manicured to fit in the yard. My mother was not one to wait for a man to make a decision that was way overdue. After all, all four kids were sleeping in one small room with three of us already going to Montrose School across the field from our home.

Mom chose a home on the southern outskirts of the town, hired a dray and moved all of our earthly belongings to the new place without telling Dad. When he finished his work at the restaurant fairly late at night, he went home to find it entirely empty of all furniture with not a soul around. Although it is quite funny now, it certainly was not humourous then. I was only eight years old, and Bill, the youngest of us, would have been four years. I cannot recall how Dad found us in our new residence so late at night, but I think it might have caused a certain amount of marital friction to say the least. In the end he adjusted quite well to the new place because it was nearer to the farm he had just leased—and he knew that Mom really had everyone's best interests at heart

Our new home was also surrounded by a picket fence, but this time it was six lots large so Mom could have her own garden on one side of the house and she could raise chickens in the garage and let them run loose on the other lots. There was so much space that we could play "Anti-I-Over" over the house and other games in the yard.

MARVIN FAMILY C. 1942

However, we soon found other things to do on the other side of the road at the front of the house. There was a huge parade square where soldiers practiced their marching skills during the war years. When they weren't using it, especially in the evening, we Marvin kids, and all the neighbourhood children, would play "Prisoners Base" or "Kick the Can" or other group games. In the spring there was a swampy area next to the parade square filled with willow trees where the boys could float and navigate their crude homemade rafts around the various tree obstacles, and sometimes fall in. On the square there was lots of space for flying the homemade balsa wood planes and kites that Jack and Bill built.

GREENHOUSES

The Farm, Market Gardens and Greenhouses

As if Dad didn't have enough to do with his restaurant, he leased a small farm from a Mr. Weicker. He started a greenhouse business that not only kept *him* busy during his afternoons off but also his wife and children after schools and weekends. The community was the recipient of the fresh farm produce and spring bedding plants that were not then readily available anywhere near the town. Most of this produce was sold to Bird's Grocery on the corner of Richmond Avenue and Clairmont Road, to Wong's Grocery where Eva worked after school, and to Wright's Grocery where Grandma shopped. I guess you could call Jack an entrepreneur because he saw what was needed and proceeded to do something about it. He and Mom were not afraid to put

DAD TRANSPLANTING
IN THE SPRING

their kids to work, and we were given plenty of chores.

The Farm that Dad leased was about half a mile from our new home, so Mom and the boys (and sometimes the girls) would have to walk there and back each day. We loved to walk across the field next to our farm where the army had an assortment of fitness equipment and obstacles for the soldiers to practice on for their military training exercises. When the farm work of the day was finished and we walked back home, (the boys especially), would play on the various military stations when the soldiers were not occupying them.

Eventually the work at the farm became more onerous, so a small tractor was bought to shuttle Mom and the boys more quickly to the hog farm, chicken coops, greenhouses, market garden and potato patch that eventually sprouted on that land. The farm operations grew larger with each passing year. While Dad was basically the master of the greenhouses, Mom and the boys managed most everything else. During the summer, Eva and I joined them to plant, weed, harvest, clean, and can the produce. We were often joined by Nieta and Grandma Wiedeman with the cleaning and canning. On our weekends, we helped clean chickens and deliver eggs on our bicycles to certain residents who requested the fresh produce of our farm. The boys, in the meantime, had their work cut out for them after school by collecting the food scraps from the various restaurants in town to feed the hogs with our trusted horses, Jim and Prince, pulling the wagon. Every other day they would collect the buttermilk from the local dairy. These were jobs they definitely did not love, but the hogs appreciated it until it came time to be delivered to the meat packers. It would have been better for all of us if the town had had an open air market like cities do now, where we could have had weekend jobs selling the bedding plants, garden produce, eggs and chickens, and perhaps even the sides of pork.

The Pony Tractor and the Crushed Bicycle
A familiar sight for neighbours was that of Mom driving the pony tractor to the farm with young Bill straddling it and Jack riding his bicycle behind. As I mentioned before, the boys were spirited and full of beans, but one day on their way home from completing their farm chores, Jack was riding his bicycle *in front* of the tractor instead of behind, kibitzing and showing off to his younger brother astride the tractor as though it were a horse. Mom was getting more and more agitated as she was a very no nonsense lady.

"Jack, get out of the way and stop doing that," she shouted.

Bill thought this was really great fun—and not dangerous at all—and reached behind his back to reach the accelerator. The tractor jerked and lurched forward before Mom realized what was happening, driving over Jack and the bicycle. Jack was more than a little shocked to find himself enmeshed in the crushed spokes of the bicycle, but he was able to get up to see the tractor with a laughing Bill and a very angry Mom in front of him.

"Now you get up and carry that wreck home," said Mom, emotional yet grateful after realizing that there were no broken bones and only minor bruises.

He did what he was told, and the badly damaged bicycle was hidden away in the attic of the garage for quite some time so that Dad would not see it. Actually he never missed it.

Fortunately, Jack was none the worse for wear because the small tractor was too tiny to inflict any bodily damage, but everyone at home was pretty quiet when we contemplated what the consequences *might* have been.

Music and music lessons

Because we led such busy lives, it was difficult for me to find time to practice the piano during the day, so I would get up early to practice for an hour before I went to school. I knew that Dad was listening in bed very carefully to these sessions because I would sometimes hear him call out...

"Evelyn, play that again. I'm enjoying it."

Music, especially singing, seemed to be an obsession for him as well as an outlet from a busy, hectic life. These early morning practice sessions were a routine for me that carried through to my college and university days when I roomed with other friends. I often felt sorry for those who tried to sleep through my practice sessions, but they eventually got used to them and often didn't even hear me. I cannot recall my parents ever requesting me to practice, so I guess I inherited some of Dad's interest in music through osmosis. Unfortunately, this did not happen with my younger siblings who didn't have the same drive in classical music as me and didn't start out with the same good music teacher that I had in the beginning. So my Dad and I had a very special relationship fostered through our love of good music.

I was fortunate to have started my piano lessons at age six from a Mrs. Smart who lived across the street from us in that first tiny house. She was English and had a wonderful way with children. I could not have had a better beginning and got the highest mark in Grade three piano in Alberta. Because we had our local church's hymn book at home, I began to learn all the hymns in it, and at age nine, I was playing the hymns for Sunday School. Nieta and I were pressed into singing for a local church radio program once a week when we were in elementary school. Dad would spend hours teaching both of us the hymns that we were to sing for that week on the broadcast. He would teach us that it was important for us to sing the words clearly and on pitch so that

EVELYN AT PIANO

people in radio land would know what we sang—a trait that I impressed on all my church choirs later in life. Even this late in life, I sometimes strain my ears to decipher the words that I try to hear from the church choirs where I attend.

It was a sad day for me when my piano teacher and her husband moved to Edmonton to run a boarding house near the Alberta Legislature. Mr. Smart had owned the Five and Dime store in Grande Prairie, but they were looking to be closer to their children in Edmonton. Their move meant that we had to look for another piano teacher for my siblings and me. Piano teachers in our small community were almost non-existent. We finally all went to a lady who didn't have the same patience and interest in children. She didn't have much trouble with me, but she would crack a ruler over the knuckles of my brothers if they didn't learn their notes to her satisfaction. That destroyed, in short order, any piano interest they may have had.

Eva's short musical career was interrupted when she contracted polio at a summer church camp and spent a year at the Colonel Mewburn wing of the University of Alberta Hospital in Edmonton, recuperating and being rehabilitated to walk again. Mom and Dad would drive to Edmonton quite often to visit her in the hospital, but she also had visits from our Aunt Susan and Aunt Helen who lived in Edmonton. I was given the responsibility of looking after Jack and Bill when they were away.

I would have been about thirteen years old. Looking after these two spirited brothers of mine was not necessarily a piece of cake, but somehow we managed to stay alive without attracting the neighbours to our shenanigans. Now we laughingly talk about angrily chasing each other around the outside of the house with one of us holding a butcher knife, but we cannot remember which one of us was wielding it. When Mom and Dad finally returned Eva home, both her legs had to be strapped into casts each day for a while. During the polio epidemic that swept Alberta, many people we knew did not survive, and Eva's recuperation was a result of her tremendous determination and perseverance that became a reflection of her whole life and eventual nursing career.

Because our new piano teacher didn't have the patience of Mrs. Smart, she decided that I should take all her beginning students because she really couldn't be bothered with them. It takes a special person to teach youngsters to love the piano or any musical instrument for that matter. In grade seven, I really wasn't that person. I had no experience, was far too young, and had no mentor to watch over me or to teach me these teaching rudiments. Because we needed the financial resources, I agreed to take about twenty of her beginning students that she didn't want to teach. What a way to learn to love teaching! I began to teach piano after school and all day Saturday, even going to the homes of some who had physical problems. It was a good experience for me, and the children's parents really appreciated it, but it convinced me that I never wanted to become a teacher to other people's children, especially if they were pushed into something they didn't want to do.

Thus ended my teaching career after three years. Notwithstanding this youthful episode, I fervently believe that teaching is one of the most important professions for anyone to pursue. Helping people debate and discuss important issues civilly, helping them gather their thoughts and open their closed minds, encouraging them to think outside the box and find other solutions for problems, inspiring young people about life... well, these are some of the greatest accomplishments to which we can aspire.

In my junior high years, I became very interested in the violin, so interested in fact, that Mom ordered a violin from the Eaton's catalogue for my Christmas present. Then began a search for a violin teacher. The one teacher that we thought we might get moved away. Finally, in desperation, Mr. Gavinchuck, my grade ten chemistry teacher, said he would help me with his limited knowledge of the violin. It was very gracious of him, but he was right, his violin skills were very limited, so I gave up. However, that squeaky violin helped me when we had to learn the rudimentary skills of violin at university and when my own children took up the violin years later.

CHAPTER FIFTEEN

Our Home Life

As I look back on our past family life with my parents, I realize that we were most fortunate to not have had an easy life. We siblings always thought we were rather hard done by due to the lack of luxuries in our home such as indoor plumbing and a phone that our peers enjoyed. It made us a little ashamed of our home. But now I know we enjoyed other things that our peers did not. We travelled all over the Peace River Country, to Edmonton and Kelowna, visiting restaurants, market gardens, greenhouses, peony gardens, and aunts and uncles in various places. We learned to eat all kinds of different foods, to behave in restaurants, to sit still in the car when we travelled and entertain ourselves on long trips when our parents were busy. We learned to keep our mouths shut when we wanted to grumble and to do things immediately when our parents asked. Hesitation and procrastination were not states we could indulge in.

We knew that our parents had their communication problems and their occasional disagreements, but we knew too that they did love and respect each other in their own way so long as each didn't have too many expectations of the other. Their early personal experiences influenced their necessity to become independent and to make responsible decisions not only for themselves but also for those that depended on them. Our mother was responsible for our upbringing and discipline. That was her job in that era. Dad was responsible for coming home to see how she was doing with us and whether it was working. He determined where and when he worked and played, but then I think other fathers were the same in that era. So many of my peers had fathers who spent a lot of time in the bars or with no fathers at all. We were isolated and protected from those situations.

However, we four children were also isolated from the outside world problems since there was no such thing as television, only one regular nightly radio news broadcast that told us about the wars that were so far away from our simple existence. In our ignorance and youth, we were a relatively happy family, albeit more hard working than many of our peers. We couldn't hang out at the coffee shops after school because we had duties to do. There was no such thing as boredom. We had too much to do and not enough time to do it in. We didn't have any extra time to get involved in extracurricular activities at school—except for the Glee Club and church youth groups on the weekend.

Our Daily Routines

Our mother was very devoted in her faith and active in her church. It gave her comfort when she didn't always like her lot in life—raising four rambunctious preschoolers in the beginning, the hard work of farm life, and precious few luxuries in the home. Like most of the women of her day, she had a regular schedule of home and farm duties that had to be done to keep ahead of the game of feeding farm animals and hungry children and keeping the house in order.

Monday was laundry day with a wringer washer, a ribbed scrub board, and an outside clothesline in summer and winter. In winter, the frozen stiff clothes were brought in after the days farm work was done and hung again on lines strung across the kitchen until they warmed up ready to be rolled up for ironing the next day.

You guessed it, Tuesday was ironing day. Everything was ironed including tea towels and bedding and white shirts and blouses—even the boys long pants. There was no such thing as wrinkle free fabrics. The ironing was done on the kitchen table.

Wednesday was baking day and further farm work to keep the animals fed when the boys came home from school. There were no kitchen cooking appliances to make baking and cooking quicker and easier. Mom had a hand beater and a large spoon for mixing. The wood and coal stove was crude but effective, and one dare not jump around or even talk too loud or open the oven door too soon for fear the cake or buns or goodies would fall with the rush of cold air.

Thursday might be Mission Circle at the church or at one of the homes of the church women, Mom rushing home to change clothes ready to take the boys to the farm with her. Then the boys did their round of daily chores. Every other day they would man the buttermilk wagon getting the buttermilk from the local Creamery. On the other days, they did the round of all the Chinese restaurants picking up the restaurant food scraps for the hogs. All of this unwanted food stuffs would be dumped into the hog's metal food containers and mixed together over a fire for their feed.

Friday was usually sewing day, Mom making just about everything that she might not have ordered from the Eaton and Sears catalogues. She even made Dad's white dress shirts for the restaurant. Mom's sewing machine was a very simple portable machine that had to be set on the table and then cleared off for meals. Her ironing board as well as her fabric cutting board was also the small kitchen table that had to be cleared off in time for dinner. Needless to say, she didn't waste much time on any one project. I hated the things she sewed for me, but now when I look at the photos with the clothes she made us wear, they really look quite good. I am proud of her now for what she did with so little. But as soon as I took home economics in grade seven, I started making all my own clothes. One special project that I made that first year with quilting patches left over from my Aunt Helen, was a lined kimono with many patchwork fans running down its front and back. It was definitely a work of art that I am sorry I did not keep, but probably it got worn out.

Saturday was a very busy day. Morning was house cleaning for Eva and I. Mom went to the farm with the boys to do the chores there. They'd then bring home the eggs and chickens for cleaning and delivery to those in the town who had ordered farm fresh produce. All of us children had to participate in one or the other of these jobs. We had to be mighty careful not to break the eggs that were mostly in a bag in our bicycle baskets. This was a very tricky endeavour to accomplish over bumpy dirt roads. Some of our old lady customers were very fussy and complained if we happened to crack one or two. Mostly though they were all congenial and grateful to see little kids doing this kind of work and being so responsible. We also had to make sure we got paid the proper amount.

When all of these duties were performed, Mom and Eva and I went grocery shopping to Wong's Grocery downtown. The groceries were delivered to our home by the local delivery man, Anton, later in the day. After the groceries were picked out, we all went to Dad's restaurant for coffee. This was always a treat for us as we loved the coffee Dad made, and it was nice to act grown up with Mom while Dad waited on us.

Sunday was for Sunday School and Church, even in the evenings. Otherwise it was basically a restful day as we weren't supposed to do too much. On our own, we would go and visit Grandma, roam the hillsides with Nieta, or go home and play games or practice or any-thing else that wasn't too strenuous. Of course, Mom and the boys always had the farm chores whether it was Sunday or not. As we got older, this restful Sunday for us kids became just as busy as the rest of the days.

While we were small children, Mom would take us to visit Grandma, Nieta, and the rest of the uncles and aunts who were left in Grande Prairie in their simple home down in the Bear Creek Flats at least twice a week. To get to their place, we had a very exciting walk for small tykes. In the summer we walked along a street with hedges that had orange and red berries which we would pick and squish on the sidewalk with our shoes—the berries were not good to eat. Further on was a sidewalk with a boarded tunnel underneath it, meant to carry runoff water, I suppose. Usually this tunnel was dry and open on both ends so that it was possible for us to walk inside it, chasing each other to see who would be the first to get to the end. Over the sidewalks and tunnel, we happily skipped until we reached the rickety wooden bridge straddling a small ravine filled with poison ivy. Here we rested while looking over the railing wondering if the three Billy goats gruff were down there somewhere that we dared not go. Our mother prodded us on, and finally we were at the top of the big hill just in front of Grandma's house. To us this was the biggest hill in the world. How disappointing to find out when we grew older that it was a mere big bump in the road. However, it provided lots of opportunity for tobogganing in the winter.

IN FRONT OF THE BIG HILL IN
FRONT OF GRANDMA'S HOME

Nieta, being a year and a half older than me, would take us on all sorts of nature adventures around her home, perhaps ending up at her neighbours, the Toews, who had a two-seater wooden swing under huge poplar trees that would seat four or five of us kids. One unfortunate incident I remember quite vividly was that I got my big toe caught between two moving parts of the swing. It wasn't a very pleasant sensation and took quite a while to heal. Other times we would wander through the sunken garden in Grandma's yard, peppering the seeds from the poppies into our hands and enjoying the taste as we spirited them into our mouths. What fun we had with no adults dictating our actions and no worries of perverts or bad people who might kidnap or harm us. This would not happen today, but in our young days we and the adults around us were ignorant of these horrible possibilities that only happened in big cities far away from our world. In the winter, we would toboggan down the hill in front of Grandma's house or play board games with Uncle Jake around the big wood kitchen table, savouring the warmth of Grandma's wood-fired stove.

The Marvin Christmases and New Year's Celebrations

It is interesting to note how the Nation's celebration of the annual holiday season has changed over more than eighty years. In the forties and fifties our Christmas did not include such an emphasis on the materialistic and marketing phenomenon we experience today in the twenty-first century. Early on Christmas Eve morning, the boys would hitch up the horses and wagon and make sure the proper tools for cutting a tree were in place and that the wagon had an appropriate amount of hay for the horses and for us to sit on to keep warm. We girls would take along blankets and lunch and away we would all go to what *we* called the Three Mile Corner but which was also called the town dump. However, it was not far from home, and there was an abundant source of spruce trees nearby for us to find our ideal tree. In those days, there were no regulations against cutting a tree down in the forest surrounding our town.

In the earlier years, one of our uncles would come along to help us and to find a tree for their home as well. Some days the weather was so cold we almost froze to pieces especially our toes. But we made it back home after a courageous cold winter adventure in time for the boys to build a stand for the tree and for the girls to decorate the tree with our one string of coloured lights and the hanging tinsel which had been carefully taken off the tree each year to be used again the next year.

Then we would listen to Christmas music on the radio and enjoy the tree lights. In Grandmother Wiedeman's home, they lighted special candles that clipped onto the end of the tree branches in the first few years until they could afford electric tree lights. I would imagine now that that would have been a major fire hazard.

A huge pile of gifts was placed under the tree after all was finished. The Chinese bachelor men in town excelled in their generosity towards all us children, giving us boxes of Pot of Gold chocolates and dolls for the girls. Mom would keep a box for each of us and give the rest away. She did this with the dolls too, but I can't remember being that interested in dolls anyway, although Eva was. The boys got model airplanes to make.

What a change from today when most people put up their Christmas tree the first of December or even earlier. Usually it is an artificial tree made in China that comes apart in three or more sections for easy storage with hundreds of attached lights on the branches that makes it a breeze for decorating. Today's gifts include every available technical toy that a child has been craving complete with the appropriate sim card or batteries needed to make it operate. It might keep them preoccupied for a few minutes or for the whole day.

At this time of year, besides the late evening Chinese dinners at the various restaurants in town, we were also expected to be at Grandma Wiedeman's for the noon-hour Christmas and New Year's dinners that she prepared for her family. This always included the Marvins. In our early childhood, we would occupy the time before and after dinner, tobogganing and sliding down the hill in front of her house with Nieta, while Mom helped Grandma with the preparations. Mostly we used bits of cardboard, but one year we got an honest to goodness toboggan. Another year, the uncles built a bobsled that was quite exceptional because you could steer it and it had two pairs of runners that allowed one to turn the sled more easily. I think they must have gotten the plans from the *Popular Mechanics* magazines that we all loved to peruse whenever they left them lying around.

One New Year's Day at Grandma's stands out in my memory. I think we had just completed dinner when Mom looked out the window and

CHRISTMAS DINNER AT THE RESTAURANT

noticed black smoke billowing into the sky from the direction of our farm. She summoned the boys to the window.

"That looks like it's coming from our farm. Get your clothes on quickly. We're leaving to see what is happening there."

So off they went in a great rush to discover that, indeed, the hog barns complete with at least a hundred hogs had completely burned to the ground. At least a year's work destroyed and up in flames in minutes while we were enjoying ourselves over dinner—a great tragedy for Mom and the boys not to say anything about the poor hogs.

In our church, preparation for the Christmas pageant began in late November when everyone from the smallest child to the oldest in the congregation had a part to play no matter how small. Sunday School children started to memorize their lines for their part in the group and to meet for rehearsal in the middle of the week. The mothers became busy with making costumes and organizing the event or rehearsing the singing of each little class choir.

The Christmas Season was very special, not necessarily because of the gifts we might or might not receive, but because we took the time to be with all the family that included Grandma Wiedeman's family and all the Chinese boys in the local Chinese restaurants. Later on as we grew older, the holiday season allowed us to attend skating parties.

Skating in those days was almost always on outside rinks or ponds until the town built a large skating arena basically for hockey games and with the wonderful addition of a sound system which meant we could skate to music.

One of my fondest teenage memories is the Boxing Day Party at the Balisky Farm where their boys would shovel the snow off the nearby creek and flood it. The Balisky family would invite people from all over the countryside and towns for this event, which would include well over a hundred people. After the fun times skating, we would all sit down at their big dining room table in shifts to enjoy a full turkey dinner with all the trimmings. They had a big family with lots of help from the Balisky girls, but even so everyone did their best to help out at this annual event that brought people together from a wide area of the Peace River Country—a community event totally hosted by one farm family to include a wider circle of people. Talk about memories of bygone years!

CHAPTER SIXTEEN

Legacy

As I ponder the legacy of my parents, I am impressed with how independent each was of the other. After their wedding, Dad continued to operate in his life as though he were still a bachelor but liked the comforts of the home Mom made for him and the children about whom he could boast. He pursued his interests such as golfing, playing pool, working in his greenhouses, and singing as though he didn't have a family to restrict him. On many Sundays, after we had dinner at the restaurant, following morning church, Dad would take us all to the Richmond Hill Golf Course seven miles west of town. In those days we could follow him around on the course while Mom stayed at the clubhouse knitting or doing her embroidery work. We loved these country rides and adventures as little kids.

Mom worked independently of Dad to create a home for her growing brood and for her husband even though he sometimes seemed to be unaware of the expenses, the work, the nurturing, the educating, the

DAD AND SANDY - THE GOLF
PRO -AT THE GOLF COURSE

clothing, and the emotions involved. Like Dad, who was an entrepreneur in his restaurant and market garden, Mom was also entrepreneurial in how she and the boys managed the farm and how she took charge in the home to feed and clothe her children. She worked hard to accomplish all these tasks and still had time to socialize with her mother and family, her neighbours, and her church friends. Early in my life, before the farm was in the picture, Mom and I would have tea or coffee visits with some of the other pioneers in the town like Mrs. Galway, whose husband we called Judge Galway, or Mrs. Putters, who had a huge chest of her beautiful embroidered handiwork that I loved to see, or Mrs. Whitlock, one of my Sunday School teachers, who gave me a mirrored plaque with a bible verse on it that I treasured so much it became my life motto.

"In quietness and in confidence shall be your strength" (Isaiah 30:15).

For years during my marriage to Tom this plaque was placed on the wall above our stove in the kitchen where I could see it every day while I was preparing the meals until one day it broke when we pulled the stove out to clean behind it. The verse stuck in my mind all these years to give me inner strength and patience when I needed it.

Mom wasn't too concerned with whether we took music lessons or not, but Dad was. He was especially influential in my early music life because he enjoyed singing and hearing me play the piano. He was fortunate to have a daughter who didn't need persuasion to practice or to play for his singing—for which he had a great love and an obsession.

Mom made sure that each of the four of us kids were thoroughly indoctrinated into our Baptist Church, and later as teenagers, we all sang in the church choir and participated in the youth group activities and shenanigans. It was a fun time for us despite the isolation from other non-church activities. When we were teenagers, our church choir would sing every Sunday at the local hospital after our noon meal at the restaurant. It was an event that taught us to care for the patients and for somebody else besides ourselves. But it was also a social event for those in the choir. I would accompany the choir on a folding portable pump organ—an instrument I have never encountered since—but sometimes the choir would sing *a cappella* [without an instrument], a most beautiful sound if everyone sings on pitch. Nowadays when we sing Happy Birthday at parties, everyone seems to start off on a different pitch, and I am taken longingly back to those days of choral singing when everyone broke out in harmony and stayed on pitch. There is nothing quite like the instrument of human voices singing as one and enjoying it.

Now that I am older, I covet that wonderful experience for all young persons, especially if an instrument is too expensive to buy. One always has the human voice as the most important instrument. To use the singing voice properly is something I shall always appreciate about the legacy Dad left me. As very young children, Nieta and I were requested to sing together in a regular weekly church radio program, so my Dad would patiently, and sometimes not so patiently, teach us the hymns we were to sing that week. Now in our senior years, one would never know that, at one time far in the past, we had beautiful youthful singing voices. However, like all muscles, if you don't use it, you lose it, and we have definitely lost it.

Both our church and our mother were quite narrow in their faith, and we were not allowed to go to dances, to smoke or drink alcohol, to wear lipstick, to go to movies or play cards. I guess these exclusions didn't hurt us, but they certainly isolated us from other friends and placed us in a ghetto of sorts. I guess my smoking Dad didn't mind either because he probably felt we were kept away from the effects of these so-called vices. Compared to the vices of today's youth, these could be considered quite minor and trivial. I do regret the exclusivity that this behaviour must have represented to others who might not have understood our parents' concerns. And of course, when we were mature enough, we made our own decisions about what was right and what was wrong in life. Perhaps a strict lifestyle in one's youth is not such a bad thing so long as one is also given a certain amount of freedom to make a choice and a decision. In the end, we are responsible for the decisions we make whether they be good ones or unfortunate ones, so our parents needed to protect us from making the wrong decisions before we had the maturity to make good ones.

Mom had learned how to be responsible as a young girl who had to help Grandma with her expanding brood of twelve other children at a difficult time. In any task she set her mind to, she quickly adapted to the challenge. When her children left the nest to further their education, she moved lock, stock, and barrel (so to speak), including Dad, to a different home when the property of our second home was to be developed for a local mini market.

Any properties that Dad leased, such as our homes and the farm, were never bought and owned by us because, in those early days, the Chinese were not allowed to own or buy property in Canada in the same manner as they were not allowed to serve in the military or to work in the gold mines in the Yukon.

While Mom raised and nurtured her children as best she could, there was never too much time to communicate about any issues other than religion and what was in the Bible. Most of us did not reveal our innermost thoughts to either of our parents. This resulted in each of us making decisions on our own about what we would do in our future or the pathways we would take to accomplish our goals. We became responsible and resourceful and quite independent of our parents in our late teens.

CHAPTER SEVENTEEN

Final Years of Our Parents

September of 1964 marked a new era in our family's life. Bill and his new wife, Donna, had begun working on the farm in a new market gardening operation in conjunction with Jack Jr. who was the major financier for it. Their plan was to continue with Dad's market garden project since Dad was reaching his senior years and had given up the restaurant life—although he still helped the other Chinese boys at the Donald Café as their front of house man.

Mom, in the meantime, had gotten a nice job at the Grande Prairie Municipal Hospital as a ward aide, having given up the hard work on the farm for so many years. She liked the hospital life and was well liked in the hospital by her colleagues there. Our parents were getting older, and their children had left home to pursue their respective educations in various fields and in various places. I had married Tom, my lawyer husband, and was raising two preschoolers with another one on the way soon. We were not able to visit in Grande Prairie as often as we had before the children arrived, and Tom's nascent legal career kept him extremely occupied in the prestigious firm he had joined— one of the oldest and most respected legal firms in Edmonton known as Field Hyndman at that time.

Dad's Accident

One afternoon, I received word from Bill that Dad was involved in a tragic accident on the farm. Bill had removed the greenhouses from their long-time location to a spot down the hill to where the hog pens used to be, the hogs no longer being a part of the operation. This spot was close to the creek bed in a well secluded and protected part of the land, but one had to navigate a fairly large hill to get to it. Dad had been working in the greenhouses there on a day following a rainy season. When he was navigating the muddy hill on his way out, his car got stuck in the gumbo muck. He walked the distance from the farm to the nearest road and hailed down a gravel truck to ask for their assistance in pulling his car out. While he was watching on the side-lines of the hill as the truckers proceeded to do their best to extricate the car, the truck slipped and ran over him crushing his pelvis. He was rushed to the hospital where he lay for three days. The doctors there did not know what to do and as a result did very little.

Finally, in desperation at the inadequate care Dad was getting, Eva and Jack travelled to Grande Prairie in Eva's Volkswagen to see what the problem was. They were extremely disappointed with Dad's doctor who sat behind his desk talking to them with his feet propped up on his desktop. This casual, impersonal attitude towards Dad's critical health and care prompted them to immediately make arrangements to fly Dad and Eva by air ambulance to the University Hospital in Edmonton. The plane landed at the Municipal Airport as there was no closer spot to the hospital at that time. By Eva's account the distance between the airport and the hospital by ambulance was one of the longest she had ever encountered as each bump along the way elicited an agonized groan from Dad.

My Sorrow

I visited Dad in the hospital that evening, but my emotions were very close to the surface, and I was afraid that I was falling apart seeing him lying there in such pain. I could not speak other than to hold his hand. I was pregnant with our next baby, Peter, and could not express my love and concern for Dad. I was so distraught and afraid to cry in front of Dad when he was in worse condition than I had ever seen him. I didn't want to break down and make him feel worse, so I did not stay long. It was too hard for me to control my emotions. Dad was taken into the operating room almost immediately, and we got word early in the morning that, after the long journey, he had not survived the operation that revealed the extent of his crushed pelvic area. It has taken me all these years to finally get over the fact that I was so weak and unable to stay with him during his final hours even if just to hold his hand and let him know what he meant to me. He had been a major influence on me in so many ways, including encouraging me to be involved in music although he did not finance any of it.

Although Dad had never been a part of the McLaurin Baptist Church, the funeral was held there with a standing room crowd including the two truckers who had tried their best to remove Dad's car from the muddy hill. Dad had been such a part of the pioneer Grande Prairie community for almost forty years. Our family was still in a state of shock at the past week of worry and grief that we had not planned a post funeral reception for the many folks, especially the Chinese, who had travelled from the far reaches of the Peace River Country to pay their last respects to one of their own. Our Dad had made them proud. Unbeknownst to us until later, we learned that the Palace Café had hosted Dad's countrymen in the restaurant that day after the service to share their stories of his many visits to their towns.

Bill, who had been present at Dad's side during his tragic accident, was quite shaken up over the whole incident, and he and Donna decided to give up the market garden project. They both had worked so hard to continue the market garden greenhouses in a new location. They were housed in a less than ideal mobile home and had just welcomed their firstborn child, Tara, into the world to care for. It had been a good run, but now this would enable Bill to proceed with plans to take architecture at university.

Soon after Dad's death, Mom decided to leave Grande Prairie and move to Edmonton to be closer to her children and grandchildren. She got a job at the Glenrose Rehabilitation Hospital and a second floor apartment about two blocks from the hospital where she could invite her grandchildren to sleep over. She still had lots of energy to take the kids to Klondike Days, on shopping trips, lunches, and all the other attractions Edmonton had to offer. Even though her salary was not great she always had enough to give each of the grandchildren twenty dollars in their birthday and Christmas cards each year. It was always quite amazing how she was able to function with her salary, to pay the rent, to take us out for meals at Swiss Chalet or a Chinese restaurant, to donate to her church, and travel to visit both Jack and Bill wherever they were in the world—Chicago, The Hague, Montreal, Oregon, Vancouver, Powell River or Houston.

MOM'S 80TH BIRTHDAY

Mom's Continuing Travels

One of Mom's travels took her by bus to Chicago to visit Jack and his wife Arlene and their two children, Tammy and Brooke. They lived in a smaller city about fifty miles south of Chicago. Jack had left specific instructions for Mom, on her arrival in Chicago, to sit tight and wait for him at the bus terminal until he arrived to pick her up. Depending on Chicago's traffic problems he might get snarled in the traffic. One could never be sure. Around the time that Mom should have arrived, we got a phone call from Jack enquiring after Mom, wondering what could possibly have happened to her. But what could we do from Edmonton? A few hours later we got another call from Jack stating that he had just discovered that there were several Greyhound bus terminals in Chicago. He would do his best to see which one she would have arrived at. While our hearts were pounding wildly with anxiety, we did our best to find out which terminal her ticket would be for but without any answers. About three hours later, we got the final call from Jack saying he had finally found Mom sitting quietly in a different terminal.

"Where were you?" she asked anxiously. "I've been sitting and waiting for you for four hours now. I thought maybe you got lost."

What could Jack say. She had done what he had asked her to do. Sit tight and wait for him. Thus ended a very frantic, nerve-wracking evening on both sides of the border.

Mom's Final Stroke

After Mom's retirement from the hospital, she moved herself through four senior's residences sometimes without our knowledge. Her last residence was at the Mount Pleasant Senior's Nursing Home. On her final day there, she had a wonderful visit with her brother, John, who was on the last day of his visit to Edmonton. Because she thought the bank was stealing some of her money, I decided to take her to the bank following John's visit. It turned out that, with her double vision, she had not seen the numbers in her bankbook properly, and her eyes showed that there was a zero missing on the sum. Everything became quite clear to me, and now that I am also experiencing double vision, I know that with trifocals and the wrong tilt of your head, you might not see the numbers properly. But while she was taking out some cards in her wallet, I noticed that she kept turning her wallet over and over in her hands. When she got up to use her walker she couldn't stand and walk. The bank called an ambulance and we took her to the hospital. She had had a major stroke in the bank. We knew that she had experienced many *TIAs* [transient ischemic attacks] during her last few years, but this was a major stroke that wasn't so easily fixed.

After a week at the University of Alberta Hospital, she was transferred to the Glenrose Hospital for rehabilitation. There she refused to eat even with the help of Eva, Bill and I. On one of my visits to the hospital, she told me that she had "seen the chariots across the river." I took that to be a biblical reference meaning that she was soon to die and the angels were coming for her in their chariots.

The doctor suggested that perhaps they should insert a tube into her stomach through which they could feed her. She said she did not want it, and we respected her wishes and agreed with her. However, on our next visit she had the tube in her stomach that kept her alive for two more years at the Allen Gray Auxiliary Nursing Home. She had a final stroke in 1997 and died a week later.

Mom was buried with Dad in the Grande Prairie Cemetery. With all of her children participating at the celebration of her life in the Zion Baptist Church in Edmonton, we welcomed all of her church friends and others who had come to know her over the years. The Church had been such a huge part of her life evident in the fact that she tithed ten percent of her small estate to the Church. Her Christian faith was simple, trusting, and sincere, and while we did not always agree with her, we respected her beliefs and the moral and ethical foundation that it provided for each of her children in our later lives. Mom's funeral was a chance for all four of us children to reflect on the lives of both our parents in a way that we did not do at Dad's memorial service earlier in Grande Prairie.

See Appendix B

As I ponder my parents' lives, I am impressed with their total commitment to each other even though they were so different and did not lead the kind of idyllic marriage that we all strive to have in our generation today. At a funeral service lately, a friend commented that she really admired our parents for what they did at a time when a mixed marriage of the kind they embarked on was so thoroughly frowned on by their community. In a small way, they helped forge a path for a new kind of society where all races, colours, religions, and cultures are respected by others to provide the rich tapestry of peoples that we have become in Canada.

Thes was the end of an era and into a new one.

CHAPTER EIGHTEEN

Trip to China (1979)

In an effort to understand our father, his birth culture and his homeland, even following his death, we decided to travel to China in the late seventies because there was, at that time so much interest in this isolated nation. During the sixties and early seventies this interest in China became a major international preoccupation in Western nations. What was happening there during the Communist Revolution for control was of great interest for Canada as well, both because of the large Chinese diaspora living here but also because of our potential agricultural trading interests. In 1961, Prime Minister John Diefenbaker created legislation that meant Canadian farmers could begin trading with China. Later, in 1970, Prime Minister Pierre Trudeau was the first of Western nations to officially recognize Communist China's People's Republic with a state visit, after having visited the country twice previously.

Also, one of US President Richard Nixon's prime goals at that time was to visit China to renew relationships with this populous nation after almost thirty years of a long absence in diplomatic relations. Although the US supported the Chinese Nationalist Party with Chiang Kai-shek at the helm, there really was very little knowledge of what was happening there after the communist People's Republic of China had taken over governmental control in 1949. Opposition to the Chinese communists by Chiang Kai-shek's National party forced his government then to flee to the island of Taiwan where his party still remains in control. As seems to be its custom in many areas of the world, the United States partially financed and supported the Nationalist party for several years without an accurate or intimate knowledge of the Chinese political or economic situation there as well as turning a blind eye to the corruption of Chiang Kai-shek's party.

This was the Canadian and American political climate towards the growing interest in China during the seventies that led me to get interested in my Chinese roots. I was also highly influenced by the interesting stories brought back by missionaries and other foreigners and Chinese citizens who had fled the country when the Communists were taking over. We became very close friends of Alice and Larry Loh, two Chinese architects who had fled Shanghai, eventually situating in Edmonton before relocating to San Luis Obispo, California. There seemed to be two conflicting opinions or versions of what was transpiring in China.

So in about 1977, I took a Chinese History class from Dr. Brian Evans at the University of Alberta that really whet my appetite with the idea of travelling to China to see for myself what the country of my father's birth was like. Tom, Eva, and I joined a three-week tour group organized by Dr. Grant Davies, a sociology professor at U of A, for about twenty-five people, one that would take us through several of the major cities of mainland China. This was after Richard Nixon's momentous trip and prior to the Red Guard scourge led later by Mao Tse-tung's fourth wife, Jiang Qing.

Dr. Davies had previously been to China with a good friend of ours, Erick Schmidt, and both had glowing words about what was happening there under the communist regime. Two of our tour group were Chinese history students at U of A and were also interested in seeing what the communist government had accomplished in China since taking power. Dr. Brian Evans' Chinese History course gave me a fairly objective foundation about the history of China and the communist movement after the Japanese War. I too wanted to see what was happening there despite my mother's grave misgivings. It was a time when all the world wanted to know the same thing. China had been isolated for so long from the rest of the western nations that, with the exception of what some missionaries were revealing, it was a mystery to most.

There were also three Americans in our 1979 group who had difficulty coming to grips with the fact that ice cubes were not available in their water glasses on hot days. China was just opening its tourist sites at that time and did not always have all the comforts that we enjoyed at home such as refrigeration for American tourists. I was just as ignorant about the amenities that were or were not available for tourists. For some reason, on our arrival, I was fully expecting to have outdoor toilets at the hotel, for I thought China would be quite primitive. Imagine my surprise and relief when I discovered that this was not the case unless you happened to be travelling in the rural countryside. Even the farming communes had running water with indoor toilets and other amenities. The hotels were not luxurious, but they certainly exceeded by far my expectations for cleanliness and comfort. On our travels away from the hotels, though, we were advised to take a roll of toilet paper in our bags.

By this time my father had died, so I did not have the privilege of talking to him about my plans and what we might expect in his homeland. My mother was very suspicious of our motives for going to China. She hated to hear of the advances of the communist movement there and the way they were helping to emancipate the peasants to a slightly better life than was normal. She was a very committed Christian and acquainted with all the rhetoric of American politics during the rise of the McCarthy era demonizing against anything that smacked of communism. Because she was more than a little suspicious of my progressive thinking and ideas regarding my Christian faith, I think she was very afraid we were going to become communists. She had her others reasons for being concerned as well, reasons I was not privy to at the time (more on this later).

The tour was exhilarating, educational, exhausting and fun. We all loved it. We saw every major tourist attraction that we could fit into three weeks: the Great Wall, the Ming Tombs, the Forbidden City, Tiananmen Square, Mao Tse-tung's birthplace in Shaoshan outside of Changsha, the silk industry and canal in Suzhou, Hangzhou with its weeping willows and beautiful lake, Guangzhou and Sun Yat Sen's memorial, Shanghai with its famous Bund, hospitals, factories, schools, communes and all kinds of cultural events and restaurants. We will never again be able to travel so cheaply and see so many sights as we did on that tour. However, we were young, energetic, enthusiastic and game for every venture. We did realize that we were being taken to the most attractive sights, but that didn't matter. It was all new and breathtaking and educational for us.

A Frightening Plane Trip

On one of our trips from Shanghai to Changsha, the plane had nicely taken flight when smoke came billowing out from the luggage racks above our seats. It was a most frightening moment. The seventy-nine-year-old lady, a member of our tour, who was sitting with my sister Eva turned to her with an ashen white face.

"Well, I guess this is the end."

I thought it was the end too. I turned to look down the aisle to see the stewardess calmly handing out candy to the other passengers.

What is the matter with her? I thought. *Doesn't she realize the gravity of our situation?*

The rest of our tour group were getting anxious too. By the time she reached me I could hardly bear her calm demeanour.

"What is happening?" I asked. "What does all this smoke mean?"

"Oh it's just the air conditioning," she calmly answered. "This is an old Russian plane, and that is what happens in their planes when we finally get off the tarmac."

Whew, what a relief! We all broke into a nervous but relieved laughter.

At this time in Chinese history, Russia and China were still on fairly good terms. Many Chinese engineers were educated in Russia. Chinese political leaders went to Russia to study Lenin's communist philosophy. They brought their knowledge back but made their own changes to suit the Chinese people and the Chinese culture. Eventually this caused a rift between the two nations, and China gradually turned to the west after the death of Mao Tse-tung and the failure of the Red Guard movement led by Jiang Qing.

Our tour ended in Hong Kong, and the first place we all headed for was the local MacDonald's fast food outlet for a hamburger. When we finally got home to Canada, we realized that, after three weeks of total immersion in Chinese culture, we began to suffer from the culture shock of being in our own country. In China we were able to leave our hotel rooms unlocked without any fear of theft. In one instance, I left some things that I wished to discard on the bed like an old toothbrush and some clothes I would no longer use. To our surprise while waiting to board our plane a messenger arrived at the airport with the discarded items we had left behind.

While we were aware that the venues our tour guides had chosen for us to visit would exhibit the best of a communist regime, we knew that other places we did not see might reveal something quite different. On the whole, though, we were impressed by the cleanliness of the country, the friendliness and happiness of the people and the sense of optimism that seemed to pervade the society. There seemed to be a feeling of pride at what the communist government had accomplished in such a short period of time in their history.

Everywhere we went, young people wanted to try out their limited English skills as well as other foreign languages they knew. It was quite familiar to walk down the streets of Shanghai, for example, and see a cluster of Chinese people surrounding a tourist being peppered with questions in the language of the tourist. Chinese young people knew that the world outside of their country was beginning to open up to them, and they were anxious to be a part of this movement away from isolationism. US President Richard Nixon and Canada's Pierre Elliot Trudeau were largely responsible for initiating this trend, and the young people of China were responding.

One other noticeable trend in this era was the great respect that the Chinese people had for a Canadian doctor, Norman Bethune, who left Canada to minister to the Chinese communist soldiers during their revolution in the third and fourth decades of the twentieth century. We made it clear that we were a largely Canadian tour group, and everywhere we went we received exceptional welcomes and gratitude for Doctor Bethune's humanitarian work in their country. Obviously Bethune, himself a person with communist leanings, had become one of their war heroes, and Canadian tourists were recipients of the Chinese people's gratitude for Dr. Bethune's work.

At this point I should explain to my readers why I am finally focusing on a short pictorial cultural heritage of my father that he had never experienced or even knew. Until recent times, this part of our shared history has most often been clouded in mystic and ignorance, and is why the last one hundred and fifty years in Canada has not understood the many great achievements and contributions Chinese culture has afforded the Western world throughout the generations. Although this ignorance was partly the result of the isolationist fears of China's rulers, the end result for Chinese immigrants to Canada was that they encountered here a completely foreign, unknown, and unfriendly culture replete with its racial hostilities, slurs, and atrocities that reduced them to a subculture of second-class citizens for a time.

The following pictorial history of some of the most outstanding sites in China—some of which have been declared World Heritage Sites by the United Nations—reveals an outstanding collection of structures and sites that have taken years and decades in the making. An example of this patience is seen in the many beautiful Chinese gardens we were privileged to see in this nation. Some rocks in their outstanding gardens were placed in rivers for years so that the flow of the rivers could sculpt the rock into a beautiful work of art. After years in the river the rock was finally placed in a garden of great beauty. Such was the patience of the Chinese gardeners and emperors. They were content to plan for future Chinese generations because they believed their spirit would live on in the after world and that they would be rewarded for their endeavours despite whatever evil they had also perpetrated in this life. Almost every example found in the photos shown here reveal a different kind of patience than what we experience in our present generation. There is also a perfectionism, a creativeness, and the sacrifice (and exploitation) of countless thousands of human beings driven by a work ethic and a devotion to beauty—and a deeply held longing to prepare for the afterlife.

Evelyn Marvin Millman

TIEN A MIEN SQUARE, CHINA

THE GREAT WALL

Evelyn Marvin Millman

Far East Meets Far West

GREAT WALL THROUGH WINDOW ON THE WALL

Evelyn Marvin Millman

TEMPLE OF HEAVEN

ENTRANCE TO FORBIDDEN CITY WITH BICYCLES

FRONTAL VIEW OF FORBIDDEN CITY ENTRANCE

INSIDE OF ENTRANCE TO FORBIDDEN CITY

Evelyn Marvin Millman

EVELYN AND TOM IN PAVILION INSIDE FORBIDDEN CITY

164

DRAGON WALL INSIDE OF FORBIDDEN CITY

Evelyn Marvin Millman

Far East Meets Far West

WALKWAY WITH HISTORICAL PAINTINGS

STONE AND MARBLE SHIP

MAP OF MING TOMB COMPLEX

SPIRIT OR SACRED WAY)

SHANGHAI BUND

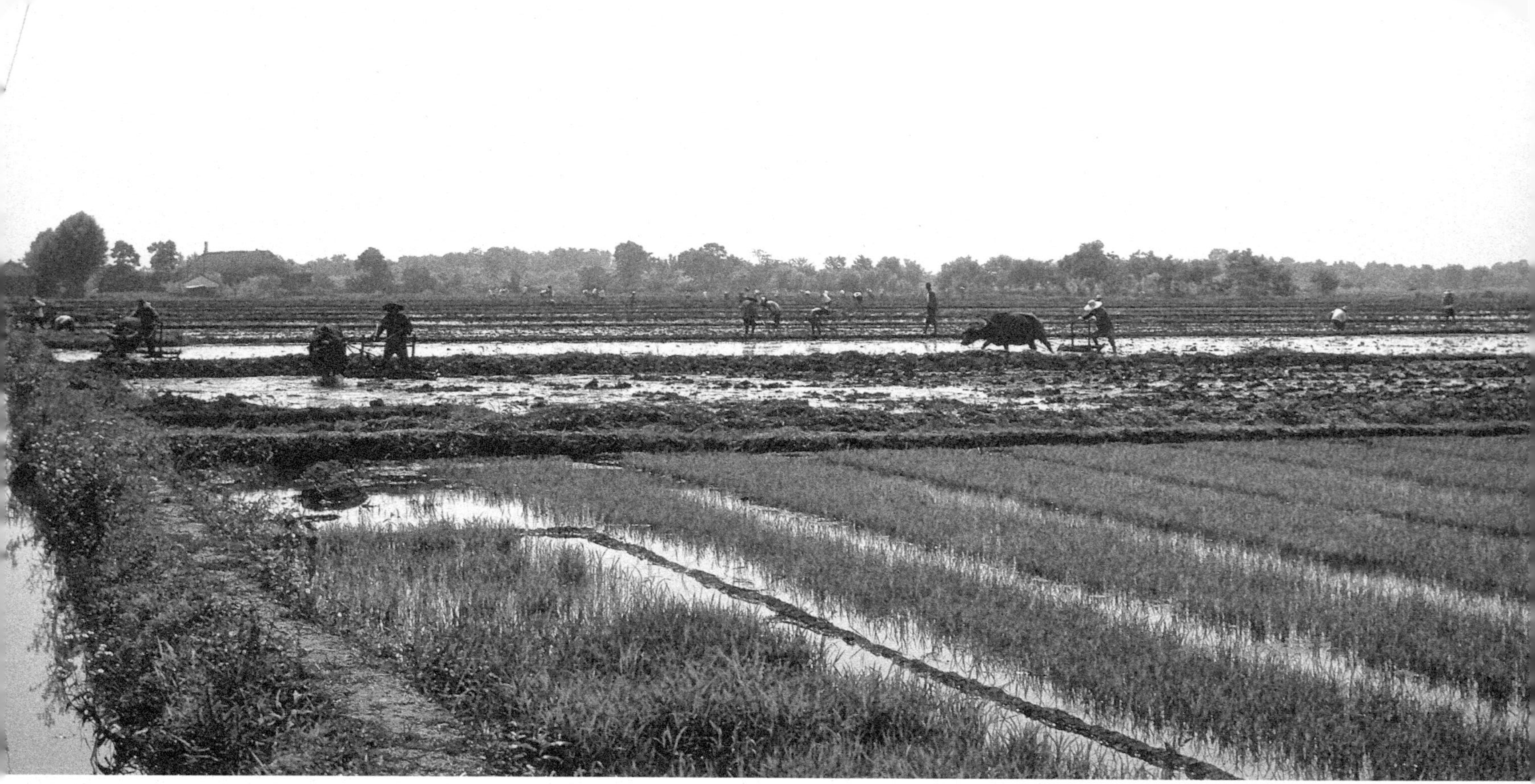

RICE PADDIE

CHAPTER NINETEEN

A Second Trip to China (1986)

Seven years later, Eva and I felt that our brothers should have the opportunity to experience what we had seen and heard in 1979 in our father's culture and homeland. In the summer of 1985, I had become a partner and shareholder in Pacific Travel with my friends Jane and Don Tsuijiura, so it was with them that I began planning my own China tour, inviting my two brothers, Jack and Bill, with their spouses, Arlene and Donna, my sister Eva, our aunt Nieta, my husband Tom and his two nieces, Carolyn and Pat Menzies as well as two seniors from the church we attended, namely Gladys Wilson and Dorothy Smith.

Both these senior gals were prominent business women in Edmonton who loved to travel. Dorothy was seventy-nine at the time and Gladys eighty-one years of age. Gladys had never used chopsticks before, but we told her that she couldn't eat in China without chopsticks. She was so good natured that she accepted our challenging pronouncement with good grace and humour and very early in the tour she had mastered the skill as well as the rest of us and was so proud of herself. Dorothy, the younger of the twosome, was a little worldlier than Gladys and somehow managed to pack a bottle of scotch into her luggage which she brought out in the privacy of the hotel room that the two of them shared during the tour. I think Dorothy also shared it with others of our tour, but I can't be absolutely sure of my

1986 FAMILY TOUR GROUP

suspicions. It wouldn't have bothered me, but I didn't know what the Chinese regulations for carrying liquor on our transportation vehicles were, so I kept quiet and Dorothy could have pleaded ignorance if she got caught.

Our tour was three weeks long, and at times quite gruelling for all of us—let alone our two seniors. However, they kept up with all the other middle aged and younger ones in our group until it came to the last day—the most important one of the tour. They elected to stay in their hotel rooms to rest and prepare for the long air travel back to Canada.

On the tour it was interesting to see how my two brothers rallied to help me along the way to do all the things a tour director has to do like administrative work, getting our seats on the plane, arranging the rooms in the hotel, booking the times for our tour bus, or getting the tickets for the various attractions we were to visit and checking all the

ROOFLINES

Far East Meets Far West

GARDEN WITH GOLD FISH

Evelyn Marvin Millman

AERIAL VIEW OF TREE PLANTING ON MOUNTAINS

arrangements to make sure they were done right. I appreciated their brotherly protectiveness towards my welfare on this busy tour and privately enjoyed their growing interest in this wonderful culture. At all times, we always had two Chinese tour guides with us—a different one for each city and one for the whole tour who remained with us for the entire three-week duration.

The Ming Tombs

This tour took us to all the major tourist attractions that Eva, Tom and I had already seen seven years ago. It was interesting but disappointing to see how quickly these sites had changed and in some cases deteriorated in such a short time. The Ming Tombs are the mausoleums of thirteen Ming Emperors scattered over an area of about forty square kilometres, nestled in a valley surrounded by three mountain ranges not far from Beijing, the present capital of China. When we went through one of the Ming Tombs in 1979, all the artifacts including, jewelry, silks, bodies, furniture and ceramic containers for burning oil, were still in the tombs in exactly the same spots as they had been discovered after hundreds of years. Each of the thirteen tombs is located deep inside a fairly large man made mountain encircled by a stone wall and large gate on the outside of a courtyard.

In 1979, the Sacred or Spirit Way to the tombs was pristinely uncluttered of market stalls and vendors except for the huge stone animals and human figures that guarded the long road to the tombs. However, in 1986, the artifacts in the tomb were no longer there. We certainly understood the importance of putting them in a museum where they could be protected more carefully, but the aura and the ambience of visiting the tombs in their original condition as we had previously viewed them seemed to be destroyed for us. Now it was merely a cold, empty structure without any meaning except for its location. Seeing all the vendors and market stalls that had sprouted along the Sacred or Spirit Avenue leading to the tombs was most disappointing. The uncluttered Sacred Way in 1979, gave one a great view of the many stone guardian animals placed at various intervals hundreds of years ago and one could not help but feel awe and reverence at the sight. Perhaps in the intervening years since 1986 the Chinese may have rectified this disturbing marketing trend on such a historic monument to the Ming Dynasty (one declared a UNESCO World Heritage site since 2003).

The Great Wall

The section of the Great Wall we visited, forty kilometres north of Beijing, was another monument to the engineering skills of a warrior people dating to the fifth century BC. It was meant to protect the Chinese people of the time from northern marauders and other warlike invaders as well as to demarcate the boundary of the regime at its prime. It seemed to us that, even though it was several feet high, it probably would not have kept anyone with aggressive intentions out very well. The Great Wall was considered one of the seven wonders of the world, and it truly is awe inspiring and breathtaking when one is standing on a part of the Wall atop one of the mountain ranges looking at the various branches snaking across other mountain tops in all directions. The other interesting feature is seeing tourists from many nations walking along its stone road intermingling with Chinese tourists who were just as amazed at this marvel of construction as we. Although the Wall was begun in the fifth century BC, it was not until the Ming Dynasty that it was expanded and completed. It was at least six horses wide with stone sentry towers every few kilometres. The structure was built of stone walls filled with gravel and topped with a stone highway built by many thousands of workers over several years. Today most of its 13,000-mile-length has deteriorated except for small portions, one of which is near Beijing attracting tourists from all over the world.

In ancient times, the Great Wall was a means for sending messages over several miles quickly from one point to the other. A horse rider would deliver a message to one of the sentry towers where it would be picked up by another sentry and again delivered to the next until it reached its final destination in this same manner.

PAGODA IN SIAN

Evelyn Marvin Millman

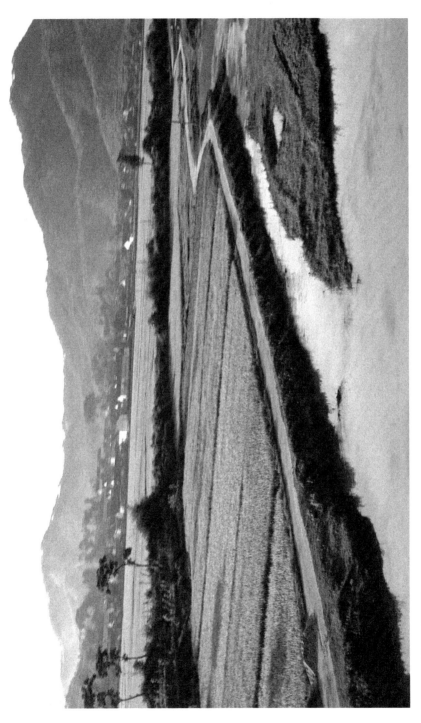

RIPENING RICE PADDY

Far East Meets Far West

Stone Warriors in Sian

Our tour this time took us, for the first time, to see the stone warriors in Sian. The site of the terracotta warriors in Sian has been further excavated since 1986 when we were there and now covers several acres of China's first emperor's stone army from the third century BC. It contains complete life-sized sculpted terracotta replicas of more than 8,000 soldiers including all the exquisite details of their chariots, horses, uniforms and military hardware of the time. It is so vast an army of sculptures as to make one marvel at the ingenuity and skills of Chinese artisans from that era and the futility of employing vast numbers of people (estimated to be 700,000) to create this monument at such an early date. Although there is evidence it was looted at several times, for years it lay buried in a vast field that was finally discovered by farmers digging a well in 1974.

The Li River and the Mountains of Guilin

Over hundreds of years, Chinese artists have painted the surreal mountain vistas of Guilin on scrolls that adorn the homes of Chinese patrons and art museums in all parts of the world. The Li River meanders like a lazy ribbon of jade through these limestone mountains that rise like pointed needle like structures trying to reach the sky. The paintings, while beautiful, cannot do justice to the actual magnificence of the sight as we discovered on our tour. The peace and tranquility of cruising down the river past tiny isolated villages and fishing boats with cormorants and fishermen catching fish on its shores vividly portrays such a contrast between that of the big city bustle and the tourist throngs that we had left behind for a day or two.

LI RIVER AND MOUNTAINS FROM HOTEL IN GUILIN

LIMESTONE MOUNTAINS AND FERTILE VALLEY ALONG LI RIVER

Evelyn Marvin Millman

BAMBOO LOG RAFT FOR FISHING ON LI RIVER

JACK AND BILL WITH WIVES ON THE LI RIVER

Evelyn Marvin Millman

EVA AND NIETA ON THE LI RIVER

ARTIST AND CALLIGRAPHY IN GUILIN

Evelyn Marvin Millman

BEAUTIFUL HANGCHOU

Evelyn Marvin Millman

Hangzhou

To newly married couples in China, Hangzhou is considered the honeymoon capital of their country because of its peaceful beauty, ancient pagodas, and beautiful lake surrounded by weeping willows. It reminded me of the Okanagan Lake in Kelowna, British Columbia, that I knew in my youth when we visited Auntie and before the extensive development that has occurred along its shores in the interim. Hangzhou seemed like a very happy place, so we relaxed and enjoyed a sumptuous dinner there with lots of laughter around our table that attracted the attention of fellow tourists in other groups who expressed their wish that they could have belonged to our group. The next morning before our departure to the next destination on our itinerary, several younger members of our group rented bikes for a ride around part of the lake.

Suzhou

This city is situated along the ancient Grand Canal which begins in Beijing and ends in Hangzhou. Its construction is thought to have begun in about the fifth century BC by one of the early rulers, originally for military purposes, and was built in stages to link the Yangtze River in Central China to the Yellow River in the north, a distance of approximately 1,100 miles when it was completed. Suzhou with its large silk industry lies near its southern extremity near Hangzhou. Suzhou is also world renowned for its classical gardens, many of which are hundreds of years old. Along with the Grand Canal, these gardens are now on the UNESCO World Heritage list.

Shanghai

During the nineteen and early twentieth centuries, the city of Shanghai was carved into four quarters governed by Britain, Germany, France and the United States in order to appease these foreign powers who were eager to foster trade with China along the Yangtze River and into Central China. Besides Canton (Guangzhou) in the south, Shanghai was a major port in China but more centrally located than Canton. If we were to go to Shanghai today, we would find many changes since

1986 as it has become a thoroughly modern cosmopolitan world city according to our friends who have visited it recently and from the reading we have done in the interim. During our 1979 and 1986 tours when we walked along the Bund—the main city highway along the river in downtown Shanghai—we saw many groups of Chinese people surrounding a lone tourist in the middle being peppered with questions about the outside world with requests to speak their language so the group could learn from the tourist. It was an encouraging sight to see this overriding interest in our particular world.

In Shanghai, as well as in the other places, we were entertained by children in schools, by Chinese operatic productions, by athletic displays of acrobatics, dancing, and singing feats. We visited hospitals, communes, farms, and factories of every description. In three weeks of touring, we became so thoroughly ingrained into the Chinese culture that when we returned home to Canada we all experienced a mild form of culture shock. In the interest of brevity, we have omitted out of our story other places with equal interest and fascination and histories such as Nanking, Canton (Guangzhou), and Shaoshan (Mao Tse-tung's birthplace).

CHAPTER TWENTY

Our Father's Village

The highlight of our whole 1986 tour—and the main reason for making this a family journey—was the long trip to the Mah village on the Pearl River Delta in southern China to visit our Dad's birthplace on the final day. Early in the morning, our small tour bus started out from Guangzhou on a modern four-lane highway. It then became two lanes, then one paved lane, a ferry ride over the Pearl River, then a dirt road, and finally a dirt path leading to a water buffalo pond. Our Chinese tour guide had left us on the dirt path to find a toilet somewhere, so we ventured forth on our own without him.

Evelyn Marvin Millman

When we came to the buffalo pond we were in a different world, with only a lonely buffalo to welcome us. Soon a few folks venturing by stood staring at us awkwardly, wondering how these people, some with blond hair, some with red hair, and some with pure white skin, had suddenly appeared out of nowhere. We could not understand them, nor they us.

On our minds when we left Canada was the suspicion that our tour guides might not take us to the right village since none of us could read or write or speak or understand the Cantonese dialect. How would we know if we were truly in Dad's village? So upon leaving Canada, we had our cousin, Sam Mah, arrange for someone to write in Chinese characters in red ink who we were, who our dad was, where he came from, and approximately when he might have returned to visit his parents. We found a photo of Dad around the age we thought he might have been on his return. This was the time to bring these documents out for our tour guide—who had finally caught up to us—to show the villagers. They seemed to understand, and it was an a-ha moment.

Not wanting to give financial gifts to the community, we had brought along two sets of gifts—musical instruments for the school, since Dad was so interested in music, and sports equipment for the village proper. The first item on our schedule here was to visit the school to present our musical gifts. We were marched along a pathway through a small rice field to the school where we again experienced quizzical looks. After our tour guide informed the school principal of our mission, he immediately dismissed classes and assembled his students in the main room where my brother Jack gave a short speech, translated by our guide, telling the students about why we were there and how pleased and honoured we were to visit the birthplace of our father.

After Jack's speech, the principal requested the students to get their band instruments and their red flag for a photo session and a march back across the pathway we had just traversed about an hour earlier. It was a simple march led impressively by the students playing their drums and

Evelyn Marvin Millman

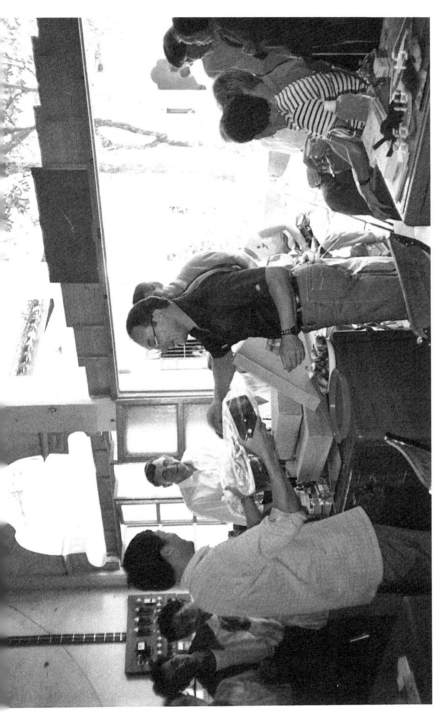

JACK GIVING SPEECH AT THE SCHOOL

Evelyn Marvin Millman

START OF PROCESSION BY SCHOOL CHILDREN

PROCESSION THROUGH THE RICE FIELDS

Evelyn Marvin Millman

LEADING TOUR PROCESSION

AT CITY HALL PRESENTING SPORTS EQUIPMENT TO THE VILLAGE

other band regalia with all of us tagging along behind towards the Village Hall. There we presented our sports equipment, and the children were dismissed for the day. We were then led up a short street to our few remaining relatives and Dad's crumbling former home.

Because we had arrived unannounced in the middle of the day, most of the male members were out in the fields or working in other jobs. Most of the distant relatives available in the middle afternoon were senior women. They decided that a banquet was in order, so while they killed a chicken and prepared a meal, we explored the street and the surrounding homes. They were very simple structures with the basic needs such as a stone hearth for cooking, a few chairs and a table, and a few pictures on the wall.

The meal was finally ready and set out on a table for the ten of us. This was a good time to show the photo of Dad, so we pulled it out and held it up for everyone to view. There was a pregnant moment of silence as we waited for a reaction.

Evelyn Marvin Millman

HARVESTING RICE IN THE VILLAGE

ANCESTRAL HOME

Far East Meets Far West

LOOKING AT PHOTO OF DAD

SIMPLE KITCHEN

Evelyn Marvin Millman

FAMILY GROUP PHOTO

Had we found the right family?

Without saying a word, one of the residents went to a picture far up on the wall, took it down, turned it around and pulled out the exact same photo of Dad which had been tucked into the edge of the back of the picture. There was a gasp as we all realized the significance of this moment. I cannot describe the overwhelming emotions and sense of relief that every one of us experienced at that time—even those who were not immediate family members. This was truly the culmination of our current China journey.

Everything we had seen and heard during our three-week trip was a prologue leading up to this moment. The chicken head floating in the soup and the buzzing flies being fanned away by the women surrounding our table no longer bothered us. This was a banquet to be remembered forever.

Our journey back to Guangzhou took only seven hours instead of the nine hours it took in the morning. Most everyone slept on the bus, but I could not forget this day, and tears still fill my eyes when I think of it or relate it to friends.

The Bombshell

As I recounted earlier, before we ever left home in Edmonton, our cousin Sam and my brother Bill and I were discussing our trip and how we would go about it.

"Will you want to visit your dad's Chinese wife's son and children?" Sam asked.

We were stunned. "What? What are you talking about?"

"Your Dad married a girl in China," said Sam, "when he returned there from Canada on one of his trips."

"I find this hard to believe," I said, still dumbfounded and incredulous.

Sam explained. "Your Dad's mother had pressured him to marry a Chinese girl, and I think a wedding was arranged for when he came to visit them. It was customary for any Chinese man living in a foreign country to come back and get married so that they could have a Chinese connection to their homeland and eventually send for the wife when circumstances allowed for it. All the Chinese in Grande Prairie thought you all knew about this, but I guess we were all mistaken."

Bill and I were still reeling to think that our father had had another wife somewhere in China and that we were totally unaware of it. However, we knew that Dad's sister was a second living wife to Uncle in Kelowna. Our Dad was happily married to our mother. Did Mom know about this? Why hadn't anybody—especially Dad—told us? This was earth shattering news that we were not prepared for yet.

Sam could tell that we'd been floored by the news.

"Your Dad stayed in China for almost a year with his Chinese wife and then returned to Canada. She was broken-hearted and lonely and finally adopted an orphaned Chinese boy during the Japanese War. His name is Paul. His adoptive mother—your Dad's wife—died of a broken heart when she was older. Paul now lives in Hong Kong with his wife and three children."

Sam knew all this because he was my age and lived in the same village as Dad until his father, Mah Yin, brought his mother and children to Canada in 1949. After the conclusion of our China tour, Tom and I spent some time in Hong Kong where we met with Paul and his family in their apartment. They were most hospitable and generous. We were glad that we made this effort to get to know this family although we have not been in contact since. They made a heartbreaking request of us to help finance the emigration of their children to Canada. We had three of our own children to educate and finance, however, so this was not possible.

We informed Jack, Eva, and Bill about this revelation and agreed that we would not bring the subject up with our mother in case she was not aware of it. If she knew, she had her reasons for keeping this a family secret. If she didn't know, what value was there in telling her now in her fading senior years. This was not an unusual custom with some Chinese men in the diaspora, especially if they had family members who felt it was important to have a Chinese connection of some sort to their homeland like a wife or a grave site or land or even a home. We all now feel quite comfortable with this incident in our father's life. I feel that Dad, who was quite fond of his mother, would have tried to please her in this matter. He tried to make a Chinese marriage work, but he had been in Canada too long and was thoroughly Canadianized to the customs and culture of his adopted land. Now we understand why our mother worked so hard to support her young family almost singlehandedly. Perhaps Dad was sending some of his earnings back to China for his family there.

As our emotional, climactic 1986 journey came to its finale, Tom and I were in great need of a tranquil change and space to assimilate all that had transpired over the last three weeks (and especially the last full day). We flew to Japan to enjoy the gardens there, not realizing that the highway traffic in Japan at that time was some of the worst we had encountered anywhere we had been in the world. When it took us six hours to get from the airport to the city of Tokyo when it is usually a forty-five minute drive, I leaned over to Tom and said, "What are we doing here?" We found some beautiful gardens where we could sit and relax without a pressing agenda guiding us.

TOM AND EVELYN IN JAPANESE GARDEN

CHAPTER TWENTY-ONE

The Marvin Siblings

The flowers of tomorrow are in the seeds of today.

William Robert Marvin – born August 1938

In his youth, my youngest brother was called Billy. It is possible that Dad named him in memory of his departed brother in China, Mah Biel, but we are not sure because William or Bill is quite a common name. Bill was the youngest member of our family, and in his preschool days, the cutest and most adorable tyke. I think it must have been lonely for him later when all three of his elder siblings left home to pursue university and college educations. He was the last one to leave home, and although he had a busy social life, he relied on our mother for friendship and solace.

Appendix A is a moving tribute and poem that Bill wrote for our mother's Celebration of her life in 1997.

Appendix C is an anecdote and cartoon drawings by Bill that he wrote

BILL'S GRADUATION FROM UIVERSITY OF OREGON IN ARCHITECTURE

of one of his childhood episodes that was scary at the time, but is quite humourous today.

Bill was probably the most artistically talented of all of us—at times dabbling into painting, gardening, cooking, building, travelling, socializing, swimming, diving, hockey, baseball, and especially using his mechanical aptitude to fix just about anything.

He was an expert in some of these areas and quite excellent in the rest. He received many trophies for his aquatic activities. His art career was promoted when he entered a contest to paint a poster for cancer. To his surprise, he won, and this helped to launch his interest in drawing, chalk, and water colours. After following his brother Jack to various work projects for Jack's companies, Horton Steel and Chicago Bridge and Iron, he got his Bachelor of Architecture from the University of Oregon.

BILL'S SWIMMING TROPHIES

Earlier Bill had married Donna Leschert from Grande Prairie, and she became his lifelong companion. With Jack's financial help, Bill and Donna decided to take over Dad's greenhouse operations at a time when Dad was in his senior years and should have been thinking of retirement from his restaurant life. However, with Dad's unfortunate untimely death, they decided to abandon the greenhouse project and focus on Bill's original plan to pursue architecture while he was fairly young even though they had just welcomed their first child into their life.

During his university years, Bill spent his summers working for Jack, welding and building the giant storage

BILL AND HIS WIFE DONNA

tanks and reservoirs that Jack designed for the steel engineering company where he worked. These interesting projects took Bill and Donna to communities all over Canada, and over the years they visited Alert Bay in the far north, Powell River on the west coast, and places in Quebec on the east coast. Perhaps one of the most interesting projects was the building of huge river channels for the Tarbela Dam in Pakistan near Rawalpindi, the capital of Pakistan. The Tarbela Dam, at that time, was purported to be one of the largest dams in the world. This project lasted for about five years, and during that time they lived in an exclusive American community that catered to the lives of foreigners who needed their own schools and hospitals for their families and anything else that would make their lives comfortable so far from their own cultures.

Bill went on to become a valuable teacher and later the Head of the Department of Interior Design and Architecture at the Northern Alberta Institute of Technology. He loved teaching and fraternizing with students and teachers alike and often organized their social activities and the department's community presentations, fairs, and fund raisers. In fact, Bill's main obsession in life seemed to be fostering the many friendships he made at work, during his travels, with neighbours, at church, and at Pigeon Lake where he and Donna lived for a period when Bill retired. Over the years, their cottage was the scene of many pleasant parties for family members, hockey players, colleagues, and bridge partners.

Bill probably inherited his mechanical expertise from his Wiedeman forefathers, and it became most valuable in my company, Envirodesigns Inc. especially in its early stages when we had to become proficient in the assembly, repair, and manufacture of our giant umbrellas and relied on Bill's help to learn what we had to do to become expert ourselves.

Unbeknownst to our family, in later life Bill discovered that he was subject to epileptic seizures, which prompted the taking of medications to alleviate the effects of petit and grand mal seizures. Later still, when medications ceased to alleviate the problems, and with new brain technology available to neurological surgeons, Bill had a brain operation that has completely eliminated the seizures. With therapy and patience, he was finally able to get his life back to normal.

Bill and Donna have two girls, Tara Lee Schiefler and Jauruey McNamara.

Eva Margot Marvin - born August 1937

EVA'S GRADUATION IN NURSING FROM THE ROYAL ALEXANDRA HOSPITAL

EVA RECEIVING SILVER TEA SERVICE FOR GENERAL PROFICIENCY

Eva was almost exactly one year older than Bill. Despite Eva's bout with polio at eight, which landed her in the University Hospital for about a year, she went on to obtain her Registered Nursing degree from the Royal Alexandra Hospital, graduating with distinction as her class Valedictorian.

Following their graduation, Eva and three of her nursing friends hitchhiked through Europe for a year, working at intervals when necessary for an American dentist at Wiesbaden, Germany, where the Allied Forces had a military base after World War II.

It was during the great polio epidemic of the early forties that Eva contracted polio at a church summer camp, a camp that all four of us went to every summer. She was completely paralyzed from her waist down and unable to walk. It was an epidemic that swept across Canada and many others were not so lucky to survive. When she returned from a year of convalescence and therapy at the University of Alberta, her legs were encased in casts that were split in half lengthwise, and she had to be buckled in for several hours each day until her legs gained their

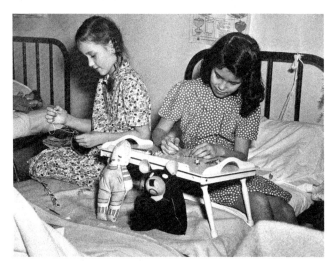

EVA AND FRIEND DURING HER CONVALESCENCE
AT THE COLONEL MEWBURN WING OF THE
UNIVERSITY HOSPITAL IN EDMONTON

strength back. Luckily she didn't miss a year of schooling as she was able to take classes in the hospital.

After a two-year stint in the Victorian Order of Nurses in Owen Sound, Ontario, and further studies at the University of British Columbia, Eva spent the bulk of her forty-five-year nursing career in Calgary at the Alberta Sick Children's Hospital, later becoming an administrator there. Since her retirement, Eva has remained active as a volunteer, especially in choosing art for the hospital.

Always good with her hands and with crafts, Eva became expert in decoupage, sewing, and quilting. Every grandchild and great grandchild received a special quilt at their birth or on birthdays or at Christmas. At the hospital where she worked for so many years she organized a group to make a special anniversary quilt that depicted the work of the hospital. It now hangs on exhibit at the hospital for all patients and visitors to see and appreciate. She also belongs to a quilting club that makes small quilts for the children of immigrant families that gives each child a feeling of being very special.

Eva became quite active in the Provincial Liberal Party in Calgary and for the Federal Liberals. Discussing politics within the family was not a favoured topic as all of the siblings had different affiliations and definite ideas, so it was easier to refrain from debating the various issues that each party pursued.

EVA WITH SANTA CLAUS
AND DEVOTED DOG JAKE

Because of Eva's charm and her pleasant welcoming personality, she has cultivated a host of friends all across Canada as well as becoming the favourite aunt to her nieces and nephews and the grandmotherly confidante of all her grandnieces and nephews who adore her.

Brother Jack was always interested in the affairs and wellbeing of his siblings. Included here are some of Jack's thoughts from a letter Eva received when she was planning to buy a new car. He had just been diagnosed with leukemia.

"It appears that you can't go wrong with either the VW Passat or the Toyota Camry. The Honda Civic or the Accord also deserve a good look. In any case, be prepared for sticker shock. ... Furthermore, it is presumptuous of me to even suggest.

"My chemotherapy is coming to a close. The cook book says that I need to be on chemo for two and half years after my initial diagnosis, which was Jan.1, 1997. With some liberties on the exact date, I expect to be "cured" in June sometime. I feel good, and I can do just about anything except remember any thing, including the time of day. I have incipient CRS, which roughly translates to "Can't Remember Shit."

Jack died in September 29, 2011 of Alzheimer's which he contracted following his leukemia.

Appendix B. Eva's memories and thoughts on her Dad.

Jack Conan Marvin – born September 1935

Jack's motto in life was "taking the road less travelled" which meant that he often took a life pathway that was more thought-provoking and arduous for him than for his peers or his colleagues who usually didn't want these difficult assignments. He was often known for playing devil's advocate in debates or discussions, believing that all sides of an argument merited exploration. These traits exhibited in his personality from his early childhood. As a young child, Jack had an inquisitive mind and a rebellious nature that was not always embraced by our mother; he had a difficult time

JACK'S CONVOCATION FROM ENGINEERING AT THE UNIVERSITY OF MANITOBA

following a plan and that didn't always fit what the rest of us were expected to do. He was most comfortable enjoying the company of those who were rambunctious and mischievous—not necessarily *bad* but unrestrained and perhaps unruly. He liked excitement and new adventures.

Jack was a year younger than me. As a youngster he had no fear. He spoke his mind without fear, and most of the time this didn't go over so well with our mother either. He was inquisitive and adventurous, full of energy, and a bit of a rebel. From the beginning, he marched to his own drummer but always with a strong sense of responsibility.

When Jack was about four during the children's time in our Sunday morning church worship, the minister was giving an object lesson to illustrate a profound Biblical message to the kids in a way that they could appreciate it if not understand. He had a hardboiled egg that had been shelled and placed atop the mouth of a glass milk bottle— the kind that used to be used before plastic bottles came into vogue. Inside the bottle was a lighted candle.

I can't remember what the lesson was supposed to teach, but Jack's eyes were wide open and riveted on what was going to happen inside the bottle. After a few moments, the candle sputtered out, and with the exhaustion of the air beneath it, the egg was pulled into the bottle. In front of the congregation Jack stood up and yelled, "There goes my lunch..." to the laughter of the congregation. He was always quick with a retort of one sort or another, and later in life he invented humourous sayings that perfectly fit the discussion of the moment. One that quickly comes to mind is "It goes over like a pork chop in a synagogue" to describe when something was very controversial and out of place.

Despite occasional episodes of sibling rivalry, we grew up in a close-knit family. We were drawn together because our ethnic heritage made us different from most children in our community at that time. We didn't always like those differences, least of all Jack and Bill. Jack was small in stature like his dad. He blamed his ethnicity and pestered Mom to take him to the doctor for growth hormones so that he would be big enough to play hockey.

Jack loved to act the older brother to his younger brother, Bill, who was too young to counter his patriarchal behaviour when they were children. Even when all of us grew older, he found it difficult to let us do our own thing without his advice and counsel, which was generally very helpful. He had a good heart and always wanted the best for each of us.

Jack had a good sense of humour, and when he and Bill got together at family gatherings or parties, they would regale everyone with their sometimes rather exaggerated tales of their boyhood escapades. Each time they related a tale of their adventures it got bigger, funnier, and more exaggerated. What one missed in detail, the other would provide, and so it would go until everyone's sides were splitting with laughter.

Jack received his Bachelor of Engineering degree from the University of Manitoba, and during his time at the university he was "a big stick" in the student residence where he resided. A big stick is one who is like a chairman or overseer of the dormitory, and the title is usually given to the more senior students who *supposedly* have more maturity than the newer students.

After Jack received his degree, he worked for Horton Steel for a few years in several places in Canada, building and repairing large storage tanks. As mentioned earlier, he also employed Bill in some of these projects as a welder because Bill could always be relied on to do a good job. Earlier Jack had taught welding at the Northern Alberta Institute of Technology where he met his wife Arlene. Later he was an important engineer for Chicago Bridge and Iron, Horton Steel's parent company in Houston, Texas. There he designed several inventions that were very useful for the company.

Jack had a voice similar to his father's, and if he had not been so busy, with a few voice lessons, he could have had quite a singing career. He sang in a men's church quartet in his youth and always had a great love for music of all genres. Later Jack was known for his ability to whistle right on pitch whenever he listened to recordings especially when he developed Alzheimer's. One evening when Arlene and I took him to a symphony concert in our new concert hall, Jack began to whistle along with the orchestra despite the fact that we had reminded him that he couldn't do that. I felt sorry that the audience couldn't appreciate Jack's condition and this new instrument begging to be heard.

JACK, JR. AND HIS DAD JACK, SR

Many times Jack showed up quite unannounced at my company's trade shows in venues all over the United States and Canada, and always to our great delight, for he was very intrigued and interested in the work we were doing in our company. He also surprised me by turning up for my senior pipe organ recital at the University of Alberta. Somehow he would arrange his business travelling schedule to include these welcome rare visits by a beloved brother.

Jack was very interested in the umbrella technology that was developed over the years in the umbrella industry to which my company, Envirodesigns, was associated. He began to envision how it could be utilized for building the tops of the huge storage tanks that his company built. Since these storage tops are generally moveable and flexible to deal with the varying levels of the liquids they contain, his idea was that a giant umbrella structure of some sort could make the building of this top much more cost effective to build. His failing health cancelled this invention interest.

JACK AND HIS WIFE ARLENE

Arlene and Jack resided in several cities during their lifetime, but probably their longest residency was in Houston, Texas. He fell ill with leukemia during his last appointment in Thailand and had to return home in Houston for three years of chemotherapy. After he recuperated from leukemia he was diagnosed with Alzheimer's, and they relocated to Edmonton to be closer to family. He and Arlene moved into a new duplex project for the remainder of his life, and Arlene became his devoted caregiver until he died on September 29 of 2011.

As I look back on Jack's life, I realize that early on it was not in his DNA or personality to follow the family line because he had a mind and an integrity of his own. This often made it difficult for him when he was required to accept the status quo. He was a responsible person in the things he was required to do, whether he liked it or not. This was so evident in the companies he worked for later in life, for he sometimes sacrificed his own personal interests for those of the company because the work was challenging and exciting. He was a loyal employee and manager. Towards the end of his life, he would say to me that, if he had to do his life over again, he would not be so unerringly loyal to one company no matter how challenging it was.

Following are some recollections from Eva following Jack's death in 2011:

"Jack was a special kind of guy! He had so many qualities that were so unique to Jack. He was loving and caring, but in his own way. At other times, he was very intense and strong about what he believed. He could not tolerate any laziness, stupidity or lack of responsibility and he expressed it strongly.

When I was teaching pre-natal classes to teenage unwed mothers along with a social worker and obstetrician, the question came up as to who gave you your first lesson on sex education. Everyone was very impressed when I said my brother Jack! That wasn't entirely true as most of my sex education came from reading books and taking courses.

Jack loved cars and, after the purchase of one car, was already dreaming of the next car he would purchase. Jack and I were driving to Grande Prairie one cold winter day. He had a huge Ford Galaxy. It was yellow.

At one point he looked at me and said, "You drive for goodness sake!"

I climbed into the driver's seat, adjusted the mirror and the seat and stretched my leg out to reach the gas pedal.

At one point, Jack opened one eye and said, "The road is no place for timid souls."

I sat up straighter, stretched my leg out further and pressed harder on the gas. I cannot remember what happened next, but I think I hit the ditch and I only hope that I drove right out again! However, Jack never mentioned the incident again!

Another time I took Jack to Kelowna to see Sid Millman, his good friend, who was dying of cancer and who wanted to see Jack. I picked Jack up from the airport with my red convertible Rabbit Volkswagen and some homemade won ton soup in a thermos. He wanted to get on the road immediately, so we stopped along the way and had the soup. He was impressed with my skill at homemade soup. The Rabbit ran well, but after its third roof replacement, it whistled especially loudly when going over 90 km. It really annoyed Jack, especially as this was early in our trip.

After visiting Kelowna and returning back to Calgary, Jack said, "Thank you very much for the trip, but promise me one thing; please buy yourself a car!"

When I decided to travel around Europe for a year after Nurses Graduation, Jack drilled me for a long time as to why on earth I would want to go to Europe for that long, let alone hitchhike. When he realized he couldn't change my mind, he drove me to Winnipeg and dropped my friend Pat and me off at the train station.

"No sister of mine is going to hitch-hike across Canada."

It didn't help that there was a rail strike on and that transportation anywhere was next to impossible, so after Jack's car disappeared, we found our way to the highway to hitchhike to Montreal, luckily aboard a transport truck full of produce going directly to Montreal, our destination where we would board the ship for Europe."

Jack and Arlene have two children: Tammy Agnew in Ontario and Brooke Marvin in West Virginia.

CHAPTER TWENTY-TWO

Comments by the Author

My readers will understand by now that Betty and Jack transitioned into our Canadian society quite well despite initial hardships and trauma as well as good times. They produced four children who left their birthplace in Grande Prairie following graduation to pursue higher educations in Calgary, Edmonton, Winnipeg, Vancouver, and Oregon. I went to the Baptist Leadership Training School in Calgary for one year—as did the rest of my siblings—and then attended the University of Alberta in Edmonton.

All four of us financed our own educations in various ways despite the fact that Dad boasted about how his children were being educated. This fact made the boys quite bitter, but I guess girls are different. I could see the value of letting your children get through their education by any means possible on their own, but it means quite a sacrifice to them. They don't have the time to get involved in any extracurricular activities on campus or to spend more time studying or socializing. There is always the thought of how one is going to get through the year by frugal means and one has to do it by taking on a full or part time job if you can find it.

In the fifties and sixties, hitchhiking was an accepted mode of travel for students when finances were stretched to the limit. The boys especially spent considerable time on the road getting to know truckers and kind travellers who picked them up for a ride to the next town or their final destination. They have some rather harrowing tales to tell of these ventures especially during their winter travels. Not willing to risk this kind of travel for girls, Eva and I had to lean on friends travelling to and from Grande Prairie to hitch our rides.

Each of us went our separate ways through our ensuing lives and careers, gathering together on special occasions to celebrate birthdays, anniversaries, reunions and Christmas. Always we remembered our unusual ethnic pasts. Somehow our Chinese ethnicity seemed more dominant than our German heritage. Perhaps it was because the European climate in Canada and in Grande Prairie was more prevalent in our community and nation. At the time that part of us blended in more seamlessly into the international fabric and flavour of our nation than the oriental side of us. Perhaps it was because we knew so little of our Asian heritage. In school and university, we studied Western civilization, not Eastern. And It was more of a treat to go out for Chinese meals than to go for German cuisine. We ate European style food at home. It didn't become special.

Evelyn May Marvin Millman - born May 1934

My brothers, Jack and Bill, could regale an audience of friends and family members with their exploits as kids - most of them true but highly embroidered with extra details that made them much more

interesting perhaps than the actual historical tale. That's the true gift of a storyteller. My sister, Eva, and I often wondered where we had been while our brothers were engaged in these hysterically funny shenanigans. I like to think that the unembellished history is equally fascinating and tells a more accurate picture of the facts, if a true story is what we seek.

My siblings have a good memory and remember little interesting details about our parents and family that I might not

EVELYN'S BA GRADUATION
FROM UNIVERSITY
OF ALBERTA, 1957

have noticed or because I was not present when something occurred. However, because I was the oldest, I was privy to things before they were born or because I understood and heard things that they did not. Because of my nature, it was always more difficult for me to seize the floor in a large crowd when there seemed to be a silent moment, so it became my habit to let others do it while I tended to other things like playing the piano for Dad or friends or helping in the kitchen. Later I focussed on my literary abilities. After years of doing all types of writing—business, letters to newspaper editors, personal, and university essays—I have come to realize that I like to say my piece on paper rather than recounting or propounding aloud because the exercise of writing seems to allow more opportunity for reflection and introspection to say nothing about accuracy and research.

However, writing is more dangerous because, once something is in writing, it is preserved whether you want it to be or not. Therefore, the writer must have a certain amount of integrity to make sure it is correct in the first place. Writing is also infinitely more work than telling because it usually requires rewriting, not once, but *many* times to get it right. It is akin to practicing the piano or any musical instrument. If one wants to get it perfect, you have to practise it many times.

With respect to family stories, in many ways I follow in my parents' footsteps. They did not talk about their lives and experiences to their children—or other family members and friends—unless asked. The day-to-day business or social occasion has always taken precedence and there are always those who are more loquacious and more interesting in their adventures.

I was born into a generation of women who still were not completely liberated in the way women are today. In our homes, we did what my young son, David, regarded as *women's work* when he was growing up. He had never experienced how hard the past generation of women worked both in and outside of the home doing men's work. It is certainly true that behind every successful man there is probably a great woman encouraging and supporting him. When it came time for a girl to choose a career, there were precious few choices available—teacher, secretary, nurse or marriage and bearing children. If you had your heart set on anything different, you had to be prepared for a very difficult journey and most likely some prejudices along the way.

All is Not Well in Paradise

There are several unhappy experiences seared into my memory bank that seem destined for inclusion into these memoirs.

When I was about ten or twelve years old, I lay awake one Saturday night when I heard the horse and wagon of the aboriginal peoples returning from the beer parlours of our small town of Grande Prairie. They clattered along the dirt road on the side of our house, as was their usual Saturday night custom, and parked in the bushes about two blocks from our home. They were on their way home to the cardboard and tin shacks at the Three Mile Corner as we called the town dump. In short order the women and girls started screaming, and I could only guess what was happening. In those days 911 had not been invented, and it wouldn't have done much good since we didn't have a house phone. I waited, thinking that someone would notify the police from the neighbours' homes, but no such luck. I cried myself to sleep, worrying about the girls in that wagon with their drunken fathers and brothers.

The second incident took place on 97th Street in Edmonton, about a half block north of Jasper Avenue by the Lingnan Chinese Restaurant. This was about 1970. Our family and my brother Bill's family had decided to go for a Chinese supper that evening. As we parked our car on the street, we noticed a large crowd gathered a few feet from our car. We got out and prepared to go upstairs to the second floor restaurant. There was definitely an argument occurring between two people who seemed inebriated in the centre of that crowd. Suddenly the man in the centre of the crowd, who was using crutches, took one of them and swung as hard as could across one side of his wife's head, leaving her stunned.

No one seemed to be doing anything, so I intervened to lead her away from the man while someone phoned the police. I stayed with her until the police came, but I myself was equally stunned with the ferocity and viciousness of the attack. All of my family including my husband and brother had abandoned me and gone up into the restaurant. I was too upset to eat, but more than that, I was so saddened that no man in my family had stayed to help me. It took me at least three weeks to get over my grief and dismay to think of the violence and abuse that some women have to endure.

I know that it is not always wise to interfere in a family dispute, but this seemed different to me. A woman had been viciously hurt, and there were enough people around to defend me, an innocent bystander, if I had been attacked. I was angry that members of my own family would not even worry about my welfare in this situation.

The third incident occurred on the street in the high end Mount Royal district of Calgary when I was walking home from a piano lesson on a mild winter day. I was about a half block from my college residence. As I was rounding the street corner, a middle-aged man approaching me opened his coat to reveal his naked body. I kept walking as fast as I could, but when I entered the college everyone could see that I was visibly shaken and couldn't speak. This kind of behaviour was not something that happened in my home town of Grande Prairie. Someone called our resident mother who calmed me down and immediately called the police. They informed me of how important it was to let the police know of these incidents so they could do their job properly by being aware of what could be an impending danger.

When our family was in Curacao on a Caribbean cruise, my daughter and I decided to do some shopping on our own without the fellows. Curacao has a very unique architecture and unique shops that definitely suggest a Dutch influence. We took in the open farmer's markets where the merchants were selling mostly farm fresh produce but also their island crafts. Then we started to window shop the stores. We became aware that we were being closely followed by a man. He was very difficult to shake and quite brazen in his close contact, so we ducked into a clothing store. While there we saw his face against the window pane peeking at us through the window. We notified the clerk and asked her if we could go out the back door to which she consented. We made haste back to the cruise ship, trying to remain as invisible as possible. Now when I reconsider our action on that day, I think I should have confronted him, with the shop personnel nearby for protection, and said, " If you don't stop following us I will notify the police." But I was too naïve then.

Nowadays we are in a different age with danger sometimes not far away. Women and girls need to be extremely aware of the pitfalls on our streets and in our communities and arm themselves with awareness

The Baptist Leadership Training School

A special year in my life was the short course at the Baptist Leadership Training School in Calgary during the 1952/53 term after I had graduated from high school. It was a time to make new friends and to study the Bible in a more ecumenical light than I was exposed to in our small McLaurin Baptist Church in Grande Prairie. It opened my eyes to the true nature of how the Bible was written and how a literal interpretation of many of its scriptures could lead to a dangerous interpretation of the true intentions of its writers.

Since its sixty-six books were written over several centuries one must consider the times in which it was written and the educational levels of those for whom it was intended. It is chock full of myths, allegories, prophesies, poetry, fables, parables and histories from which one can learn about how to live one's life and how to learn from the mistakes of history. We learned to focus on the life and teachings of Jesus that led to the Christian movement in the world today.

It was a life-changing and eye-opening experience for all the students, and I attribute that to the wonderful, learned principal and teacher of the school, Dr. Ronald F. Watts, who really never received the honour he deserved before his death. For me, it was a freeing experience to search for my own truth in a world where most institutions exact a repressive line from their adherents in order to keep individuals loyal to their cause whether it is the church, the corporation or business, the political party or media, or even the family. Loyalty to any cause should arise from the sense of freedom to express and debate one's ideas and thoughts openly in an honest and discerning environment. It is certainly not easy to search and find your own truth in today's world with so many competing philosophies vying for our attention and loyalty. The guiding line should always be whether any thinking or course of action is good for an individual as well as for the common good of mankind.

I vividly recall that school year; I financed my piano lessons with a small bursary of a hundred dollars I received from the Government of Alberta following my Grade Nine piano exams. I took piano lessons from Madam Phyllis Szeliga at the Mount Royal College, a truly excellent teacher from Poland. I learned so much from her in that year as I prepared for my Grade 10 piano exams. She made me play in the Calgary Music Festival, and when my year was finished at the school, she tried her best to persuade me to stay in Calgary with her so we could continue learning together. She offered to give me free room and board and free lessons because she could see that I was quite penniless. What an excellent opportunity I gave up to go back to Grande Prairie for the coming year to find a job before going to university. I often wonder what a different decision would have had on my life. But as with all life's choices, I closed that door and went through another for better or worse.

I have thought of Madame Szeliga often during the intervening years as she had become one of the monumental influences in my life. She taught me how to break down and analyze a composition into smaller parts to perfect and understand the whole. This is also what we can do in our everyday life. If we only look at the whole picture, we might get overwhelmed and impotent with the immensity of it all. I often have used the picture of a dirty house that needs cleaning and one doesn't know where to start cleaning, it seems such a big job. Start in one corner and finish it and then attack another section. Soon the whole job is completed.

This was my wonderful year in Calgary, and though my father thought I was making a big mistake by going there in the first place, it turned out to give me an enlightened maturity that he appreciated later. He ended up by suggesting that all my brothers and sister follow in my footsteps, which they did. Following this year, I returned to work at the Singer Sewing Machine company in Grande Prairie for one year and then embarked on the road to my first degree at the University of Alberta and finally marriage to Tom Millman.

I met Tom Millman in Edmonton when my brother Jack and I attended the wedding of Tom's brother Earl, an event at which Tom

played a trumpet solo. Jack and I had just relocated to Edmonton so that I could attend the University of Alberta and so that Jack could complete the last course in his senior matriculation while working at Eaton's and various other jobs. With a close friend, Elisabeth Schmidt, who I had met at the Baptist Leadership Training School a year earlier, we rented two small rooms and shared a teacher's home fairly close to the university. My six-month encounter with Lis at the leadership school led to a sixty-five-year friendship. None of us had much in the way of financial resources, but we managed somehow by taking part time work when we could get it. For me it was the university library and the post office during the Christmas rush. During the summer, most of my siblings and university friends worked at the Gainers Meat Processing Plant where the pay was more lucrative, enabling us to finance one more year of university.

TOM AND EVELYN ON
WEDDING DAY

Tom was completing his second year of law, and both of us attended the same church and the same young people's group there. Our friendship and interest in each other really began when Tom offered to lace my skates at a skating party and then walked me home afterwards. Following my convocation with a Bachelor of Arts degree we decided to get married after he completed his articling at the Field Hyndman Law firm the next year. Tom was instrumental in helping to initiate two important institutions in Edmonton. The first was the E4C (The Edmonton City Centre Church Corporation) that united all the City Centre churches to pool their charitable caring endeavours in one organization in which they would all participate eliminating the over-lapping of resources. The other institution was the Mustard Seed Street Church that would minister to people on the street who would not feel comfortable in the so-called straight church.

Our happy forty-six-year marriage was blessed with three children: David, Margot and Peter. Tom died in 2004 after twelve years of coping with Parkinson's Disease and after a very successful forty-one-year legal career at the Field Law Firm where he became one of the senior partners.

In 1976, when my children were in their teens, I returned to university to expand on the Bachelor of Arts I had obtained in 1957. There was still a stigma in my own family, especially my mother, around why a woman would want to do this. As most people saw it then, you were either bored with life, tired of being someone's mother or someone's wife, going through a life crisis of some kind, trying to recapture your youth, 40TH WEDDING ANNIVERSARY DAY or going through the menopause. I thought I was none of these things as I had been actively involved as a volunteer in day care, community activities, the Royal Canadian College of Organists, and in church activities, but at the time there seemed to be no thought that a mother had a life to live outside of her family because that wasn't the prevailing culture then.

Once my family became used to the idea that they might have to make their own breakfasts and lunches and a few other duties they weren't used to, they eventually became my greatest supporters.

I realized that I had allowed myself to become their servant in the first place because their lives were so busy with homework, figure skating lessons, hockey, softball, piano, violin and drum lessons that they didn't have time to learn how to do household jobs. To be fair to myself and Tom, their activities required a great deal of chauffeuring, coaching, teaching, and helping on our parts.

Now with all this busyness in our home, who would tend to the details of the home activities such as making meals, shopping for groceries, housecleaning and laundry other than mother. How different I was in raising my family than the one of my youth where everyone had to lend a hand to just keep bread on the table. If you wanted to do anything else, you were responsible for finding the time in between your family responsibilities. When I finally convocated with my Bachelor of Music in Pipe Organ Performance in 1984, at the age of fifty, I did so alongside my son David, who received his Bachelor of Arts in History. Everyone in my family, including Tom, my lawyer husband, was as proud of me as could be. It was the beginning of a new and exciting life for me in business not music.

ONE OF ENVIRODESIGN'S GIANT UMBRELLAS. THIS ONE WAS
AT OUR HOME ON LANSDOWNE DR. IN EDMONTON

Envirodesigns Inc. was unexpectedly born out of a financial venture I invested in with others—one that didn't seem to be going anywhere at the time. With my husband's blessing I took over in a new company venture, and for the next twenty-five years, my life took a different and extremely exciting turn. With the sale of my company in 2008, I began to try and accomplish all the items on my so-called bucket list that got pushed aside in the interim—the writing of these memoirs being one such item.

ENVIRODESIGN'S UMBRELLA BOOTH AT A SEATTLE TRADE SHOW

Three years following Tom's death I had the good fortune to marry another wonderful man named Frank Kobie. He was a neighbour whose wife had died of cancer. He had a varied career in the Royal Canadian Mounted Police in several Canadian cities and towns. After his retirement from the RCMP, he received his MBA in Business Administration and then worked for several years at the Accounting firm of Touche Ross in their bankruptcy department. One of the clients that he helped to rescue and restructure was the ailing oil

FRANK AND EVELYN SHORTLY AFTER THEIR MARRIAGE

company, Dreco Energy, headquartered in Edmonton, Alberta. After their successful restructuring, he was appointed their CEO for several years before finally retiring to run his own business for a few years. As with my marriage to Tom, my marriage with Frank was also marked by many travels and cruises to different parts of the world while continuing to maintain a cozy home and garden in a senior's complex.

All four of the Marvin siblings, despite lengthy separations, remained a close-knit family who loved to remember our earlier days and the good times as well as the hardships from which we felt we had survived in very good order. Our various spouses and in-laws have added a further dimension to our family which we appreciate. We have all tried to continually create family memories and reunions that we, as well as our children, could cherish—some of whom might have been too young to remember at the time

There are many fun times that we recall, such as the family gatherings with Tom and Jack reciting poetry they remembered from their high school days, each of them filling in lines that the other might have forgotten; the one non-white Christmas we all spent in Houston, Texas, at Jack and Arlene's home; the many parties we attended at Bill and Donna's cottage at Pigeon Lake where the younger ones flew aloft in the sky above the motor boat; our twenty-fifth and fortieth wedding anniversary weekends at our home on Lansdowne Drive, Edmonton, which no one would dare not to attend; the dim sums and Chinese dinners that always characterized any get-togethers, to name only a few of our many social events.

Our unique parents gave us as good a start in life as was possible during those times following the Great Depression of the so-called dirty thirties and beyond.

We had a good roof over our heads, plenty to eat, wonderful aunts and uncles, and Grandma Wiedeman to help our mom and dad nurture and coddle us *Marvin brats*, watching over us and keeping us from going astray in life. The great relationships we maintained and fostered as siblings later in life, following our post-secondary educations, various careers, and travels, kept us close knit as a family. While sitting on the picket fence of our first home, or weeding

MOM AND DAD WITH DESOTO CAR IN ABOUT 1956)

the vegetables on Mom and Dad's farm, or while the boys were feeding the hogs, or the girls were delivering eggs to patrons in the small town of Grande Prairie, we could never have dreamed in a million years where our lives' journeys would take us. We wish that our parents could appreciate now where our lives' pathways have led.

While each of us is responsible for our decisions and choices in life, we owe our genes, our values, our upbringing, our enterprising spirits, and our resilience and resourcefulness, as well as our spirituality, to the examples of these two people who gambled on marriage, didn't let hardships make them powerless, ignored prejudice and uncertainty and kept on motoring through everything that life handed them. May the next generations search and find the same attitudes in the pathways they choose. May they have the courage and the same opportunities to open the doors that present themselves along their life's journeys.

MAIN STREET OF THE TOWN OF GRANDE PRAIRIE IN THE 1900S

GRANDE PRAIRIE, ALTA.

Evelyn Marvin Millman

POSTLUDE

Dear Reader, in a Christian worship service, funeral, or convocation (or any other important audience event), the postlude might be a musical piece played on an organ or piano or by a symphony that usually ends the service or program. It is a stirring, joyful composition that acts as a sort of exclamation mark to what has gone on before. This postlude is my way of putting a final note to these writings that dwell on the important aspects and events of our family's life especially those of our parents. They are by no means complete.

Although each of the Marvin children left Grande Prairie to secure their various postsecondary educations, careers, and families, we feel a special fondness for our birthplace with its ups and downs, its hardships and happy times, its failures and successes, and its nurturing and maturing opportunities.

Our nation too has undergone the same social and maturing processes as individual families, which makes us proud to call ourselves Canadians. We have all had the freedom to do this. Ours is a continuing saga that mirrors that of many other families in this wonderful country and for each of the families that is privileged to come here.

At the beginning of this story, I mentioned that the extended families of Marvin (Mah) and Wiedeman now include many different ethnic origins, cultures, colours, religions and languages. We represent the best of what is Canada. Every new immigrant to this nation will undergo a difficult and similar journey here with what I hope will be with encouragement and applause from the rest of us. Like the

Marvins, the second and third generations will be the major beneficiaries for what our forebears dreamed, yearned, sought and earned.

Thank you for reading and sharing this historical journey into the Marvin past.

VIEW TOWARDS GRANDE PRAIRIE FROM RICHMOND HILL SEVEN MILES WEST

Evelyn Marvin Millman

APPENDIX A

A Tribute to My Mother

by Bill Marvin

Some glimpses of my mother. She was
Mrs. Marvin to some,
Betty to others,
Mother, Mom or Grandma to some of us.

This last year, and definitely the last few months, have been difficult
for Mom to communicate because the stroke had affected much of
her body! At the end, only the right hand and arm were functioning.
But she and I had found a way.

I would grasp her warm hand to say, "Hello..." and that warm hand
would comfort me like it had so many times in my life.

As we parted she would say, "Goodbye..." with her right hand.

Over the years those hands have said and meant a lot to me and I'm
sure to many of you.

They were working hands
From her earliest years, Betty was doing chores and helping out. Being the eldest child it just seemed her role. At a young age, the jobs outside the home were to help support the family, and when Dad and she started their own family, it demanded a strong, energetic wife and mother who could do many things.

They were teaching hands
Her example in work and play would help others to know what to do. They guided me in many ways...because as a naughty boy I often felt those hands to straighten me out. Even now I can still see her hand...with two fingers...and her voice... "Now Billy, you know better than that!"

Yet they were friendly hands
Mother was never too busy or rushed to stop and put her arm around a child or friend and offer a word of hope or encouragement. Nor were those hands ever too empty to dig a little deeper to give to those who maybe were more in need than she.

And Mom's hands were worshipping hands
Most of us know that her life was dedicated to that day when she would meet her Lord. She was steadfast in devotion, worship and prayer to the end.

Evelyn Marvin Millman

So some quick glimpses of those hands were:

To milk the cows, to stoke the fire,
to throw a ball, to scold a daughter,
to say hello, to shovel snow.

To write a letter, to change a baby,
to pick a flower, to gather eggs,
to follow a scripture, to draw a picture.

To give an offering, to lift a bale,
to darn some socks, to do the dishes,
to hammer a nail, to carry a pail.

To harness the team, to spank a boy,
to pluck a chicken, to weed the garden,
to swat a fly, to say goodbye.

To hang out clothes, to cook a meal,
to sew a button, to mend the fence,
to wipe the table, to clean the stable.

To hold her Bible, to feed the pigs,
to pour a coffee, to comfort a friend,
to wipe a tear, to say a prayer.

One last image I have of mother is
her hand reaching up to the hand of her Lord.

APPENDIX B

My Memory of Dad

by Eva Marvin

I really admired my Dad. He was such a hard worker even into his seventies. He loved music, and we would often see him at the piano pecking away with one finger. He wasn't a religious person, but he was very spiritual. I know many people were always praying for him, but I must say I appreciated his spirituality. I sensed that he had a strong feeling about the earth. He didn't speak a lot about his feelings on things, but somehow or other we did get what he thought about education and religion anyway. I don't remember Dad giving us any money for our education, but I guess he thought we would manage like he did as a new immigrant.

Dad was a really significant part of the community in many ways. He was well known and was often invited to sing at community events especially ones held at the Capital Theatre, songs like "Oh Danny Boy," "Trees" and "Bless This House" were ones that I remembered. At some events he donated flowers from his Marvin's Gardens like the geraniums lined up along the stage. I don't remember this, but I remember reading about it in the *Herald Tribune* ten to twenty years ago. The first movie I ever saw was with Dad called *Que Sera Sera* with Doris Day. I really liked it.

Evelyn Marvin Millman

Dad liked to golf at the Richmond Hill Golf Course often with prominent people from the community. He golfed on Sunday afternoons, and we went with him and looked for golf balls or picked berries. Most of all, I liked having lunch in the golf course lunch room. It was mostly sandwiches but served on very elegant china. When the golf course closed, Sandy, the manager, gave some of the plates to our family as souvenirs. I still have mine.

In February and March each year, Dad spent hours examining the seed catalogues to plan for the planting at the greenhouse and garden. He was a gardener. His garden was a thing of beauty. He used a huge ball of binder twine to make beautiful straight rows, leaving room to walk between the rows. When watering the plants, Dad said "Water around the plant and not over the leaves." For lunch, I would wrap a radish, a carrot and an onion in a lettuce leaf, cleaning the vegetables by swishing them along the carrot tops. It was delicious. Dad loved spinach especially when it was young and green. Sometimes he and I would poach an egg along with the spinach. I loved it.

Dad was an expert at growing tomatoes in his greenhouses. The tomatoes were all neatly tied up to the ceiling and pruned so that you could see all the tomatoes ripening. They also tasted like tomatoes should.

In the spring, people came from miles around to buy bedding plants. It seemed the same people came year after year because Dad had the best plants. He also told them just how to plant and water the plants to get the best bloom, but I know he didn't charge much for the expertise he gave. He worked very hard, and sometimes the jobs were back-breaking. At times he would lie on the floor and ask me to rub this god-awful smelling Chinese liniment on his back. I guess it helped!

Dad loved potatoes and in the fall, all of us plus Nieta would gather up the potatoes behind the potato digger. It wasn't my favourite activity, but I do remember that Dad brought us treats like watermelon and cantaloupe.

In July 1945, I was in the hospital at age seven years and about to turn eight. I was quarantined for three weeks because I wasn't feeling well and kept falling on my knees, and the doctors were not sure what was causing it. Dad used to come to see me and bring me chocolate bars. He had to sit on a chair at the door to talk to me. After my three weeks, I went to Edmonton to the Colonel Mewburn Hospital for rehabilitation to learn to walk again. In the spring, Mom and Dad came to pick me up with Dad's new car, a shiny grey DeSoto, the only brand new car he ever had that I recall.

We had some very old chairs and a chesterfield in our home. The four of us children decided one day to buy some new ones that Mom really liked. Dad was very unhappy and insisted that his particular chair be brought back.

Dad had a most wonderful laugh. It was a delight to hear him laugh out loud because it was very infrequent but extremely contagious. He would put his head back and laugh loudly from the bottom of his stomach with everyone around him laughing too.

Often our whole family would drive to Edmonton to see Aunt Helen and Aunt Suzanne. The roads were not paved, and the gravel made for a very dusty, bumpy trip. By the time we managed to arrive, we kids were very rambunctious. I can remember when Dad dropped us off, we ran up to the front door and leaned on the doorbell. By the time Aunt Helen arrived at the door, she was furious! It left us a bit deflated, but not for long. She made sure we all had a good bath to remove the dust and dirt before we could do anything.

Dad left almost immediately to visit the Lingnan Restaurant and his friend Phillip Pon, the owner. The only way Dad would remember how to get back in the evening would be by way of landmarks, and on one occasion he had to stay at a hotel because the landmarks had changed from the last time he was there.

Along the way to Edmonton, Dad would visit all the Chinese people in High Prairie, Valleyview, and other towns we passed. On one visit, it was the Full Moon Festival, and a Chinese man gave me a moon cake, and I tasted it and didn't like it. When I was outside, I threw it over the riverbank. It's the first time that I remember Dad ever reprimanding me. He was not pleased with my lack of respect that I showed. Dad was definitely the Goodwill Ambassador to the Chinese men who were running cafés, greenhouses, and laundries without the help of their families who were still in China.

I do remember saying to Dad, "One day I'm going to go to China," and he said, "Why would you want to do that!" I think he really wanted us to be well integrated and educated in Canada, and by then, he also was very integrated into the Canadian way of life himself.

On Sundays after church, we would often go to Dad's restaurant for lunch. Dad would always ask me what I would like for dessert and I would always say, "Boston cream pie." I never did have any because Mom said it was very time consuming to prepare and, therefore, was reserved for paying customers. However, I still continued to ask for some.

When all of us kids left home, it was always a big occasion when we came home for the holidays. Dad never said, "Hello" or "How are you?" but "Are you hungry?" He would then head to the café and bring home tall tins of soup or other Chinese food. He was a good cook, and I can't remember not liking anything he cooked. Often there might be strange things in the soup, but Dad would never give a name to them. He would just say, "Go ahead and eat."

There was always a Christmas party at the café, and Mom and the rest of us were always invited. As small children, we ran around a lot. We always loved the shrimp in tomato sauce, and it was not difficult for us to polish them off within minutes! The Chinese would eat all night and simply keep warming up the soup and drinking whiskey.

For Christmas, Dad made many fruit cakes at the restaurant, which he nicely decorated for the season, to give away to customers and friends, sometimes along with a turkey. I do remember that the minister of the church always received one. Mom and Dad always competed to see which one of them could make the best fruit cake. It was a fun competition that always resulted in hearty laughs on both sides.

Dad didn't want me to go into nursing as he felt the career was too subservient, and that is why he never let us be waitresses in his café. However, he sat in the front row very proudly as I gave my valedictory address. As well, when I received the honour of the silver tea service for General Proficiency and introduced him to my teachers, he was clearly very proud. Dad did not give me any gifts, but he always gave flowers. At my nursing graduation, he sent flowers and the card read:

J. Marvin (Dad).

I still have the card.

It was a very sad day when Dad was in a car accident at the farm. He was run over in the mud where his car got stuck. Jack and I drove to Grande Prairie in my Volkswagen bug when we heard that Dad was hurt. When we arrived, we met with the doctor who spoke to us with his feet elevated on his desk. I knew immediately that he was "bad news." However, he arranged for Dad to be sent to Edmonton on an air ambulance immediately. I accompanied Dad, and he was almost immediately sent to surgery because his bladder was severed and urine was seeping into his blood stream causing septicemia. He was conscious enough to know that I was there with him.

Shotgun Sunroof
Story and Cartoons

by Bill Marvin

SHOTGUN SUNROOF

Sometimes when we look back at a day in our life, we wonder how such a beautiful day with everything looking lovely, and we are feeling lively and great, could turn out so awful. The word awful can be compounded by the fact that I am only ten years old at the time and do not fully understand how my feelings run, let alone how other people react to things, or what is important and what is irrelevant.

It was early fall and the colours of autumn were everywhere. It must also have been a Sunday because the chores on the farm were minimal that day. But for me the big excitement in my life at that time was Dad's new car. I guess I call it Dad's car because we never had a car before. I think Dad owned a car before the war, but because of gas rationing, he couldn't buy gasoline. When Dad rode a bicycle we called it Dad's bike. Now he drove a car—therefore, Dad's car. This brand new thing of beauty was probably bought two or three weeks earlier. Maybe our harvest had paid off that time for a change!

In all my years to that point, I was very interested in machinery and mechanics. I'd seen cars and trucks, tractors and trains, steam engines and combines, and all kinds of other fascinating equipment that seemed wonderful but that we didn't have or couldn't afford. It all was more interesting to me when I would think of how these machines could make my world so much better. Having a machine do some of my work seemed wonderful, especially when we did all chores the old way, by hand. My brother Jack was also keen on what machines could do and why we should have some for the farm. Whenever we were doing our chores, Jack would be talking about how this truck or that tractor was better than another model and what we should have and so on. Speed was something we wanted in our world (and not how fast we could work) especially when we were behind two huge work horses for most of our chores. They move only as fast as they want, and two small boys were not going to change that. The proximity of our house and farm to the army barracks was another reason for my heightened interest in machines. There were so many jeeps and trucks, guns and shells, and all sorts of other army equipment coming and going.

It was at that point I fell in love with this new thing in my life—a brand new 1948 DeSoto car. My parents, I'm sure, had to tell me that "No, you cannot sleep in the car." It smelled so good. It had shiny paint and chrome everywhere and lush seating for six people (and I'm sure ten or more if we tried). It was powerful and quiet. It started at the turn of a key. The whole thing could be locked up tight. It was easy to steer (I think). You didn't have to pedal, and you didn't have to harness it. It was fast; from the farm to downtown and the café took only ten minutes. It had a heater and windshield wipers and headlights and turn signals. It had so many things and could do so much that all I wanted to do was drive it (someday maybe) but at least spend as much time living, riding, shining and enjoying this beautiful car.

For some reason that Sunday, I was riding with Dad in his new car. It was the early afternoon. We had come from Dad's restaurant where we probably had Sunday lunch with Dad—one of the few times in the week that we saw him because he ate all his meals there. Mom and the rest of the kids must have gone back to church because I was the only one besides Dad in the car when we drove to the greenhouses. One of Dad's café partners, Tah Soak, was with us. Soak means uncle, and Tah was his given name. Others referred to him as the "Slim Cook" because he was so thin, or Mah Tah. Dad had four other partners in the restaurant, all from an extended family. So they were all Mahs: Mah Jack, my Dad; Mah Tah, my cousin; Mah Yin, the Fat Cook as we called him; and Mah Bing; and Mah Hee. As a kid, I had a hard time trying to figure it all out. So I probably never bothered until I came back years later. Most of them didn't speak much English anyway, and that is all I was supposed to speak. But on this Sunday as we drove to the farm Dad and Tah Soak were jabbering away in Chinese, and I was sandwiched between them in the front seat. I really didn't care what they were talking about because I was so engrossed in the many neat things of this new car.

I'm sure now, when I look back, Dad was kind of showing off his new form of success. And well he should because it had been many years since he had a car and, secondly, things were coming together for him. Tah Soak had probably hardly ever ridden in a car because of being in China. How Dad got saddled with me I don't know because that was usually Mom's job. Anyway there I was a tiny ten-year-old kid (very small for my age) trying to take everything in except what they were saying. I couldn't see over the dash and when I did struggle to get more height, Dad's right arm forced me back down as though I were a bug. He didn't even interrupt his talking or conversation.

We finally got to the greenhouses. There was some discussion between Dad and Tah Soak in Chinese, and I was told to "stay in the car" with Tah Soak. That was fine with me because normally when I was at the farm and greenhouses it meant work or chores. So to be allowed to experience more of this machine was right down my alley. I couldn't see much from my vantage point in the middle of the front seat, so I maneuvered myself until I could see Dad go into the green-house for something, I presumed. I was fiddling with this, or finger-ing that, trying to get as much as I could to satisfy my curiosity. Tah Soak was also visually exploring around the inside of this beautiful machine. He turned his head to look around the back seat and rear of the inside. I saw his gaze stop on the 12-gauge shotgun lying on the rear seat. I guess Dad had gone hunting for duck and geese or was going later. After his glance, he made some kind of comment to me and I must have understood him to say, "Can you shoot a gun?" - kind of a dumb comment to make to an energetic aspiring ten-year-old boy. It was like a challenge that took me only seconds to respond. I was out the driver's door in a flash and had the rear door open—the door opens frontward and is called "suicide door." Here, someone had talked to me! And asked an interesting question about what can I do. My brain was saying, "Let me show you what I can do." Besides I *had* shot guns before while out with my brother hunting hawks and owls and weasels and any other thing that preys on our chickens. I didn't hesitate. All in one motion I picked up the 12-gauge shotgun, pumped the pump handle, and pulled the trigger. Gun safety had never been formally taught to us. It just seemed that with the continued use of guns around the place that such things would be learned and dis-cussed. As a ten-year-old boy, I was showing off trying to say, "Yes I am big enough to shoot a gun. Here let me show you."

Never in my wildest dreams can I remember being so surprised as when that shotgun blast let go! I was standing in the open door of the back of the car where I had picked the gun up. Tah Soak was in the front seat looking over at what I was doing. The tip of shotgun barrel was maybe two feet from his head when the blast came. From there everything seemed to happen in stopped time in my memory. A 12-gauge gun has powerful kick, and for a small ten-year-old boy, it was enough to pick me up and fling me backwards a ways. Besides the force of the gun blast kick, the surprise floored me as well. I was on my back with the smoking gun laying on my lap when I looked into the car. Smoke from the exploding gun powder filled the interior and there were pieces of shell wadding floating about and around Tah Soak's head. When I looked through the smoke I was surprised to see a picture I'll never forget. Tah Soak's face and two eyes were as big as golf balls planted in his eye sockets straining to see what had just happened.

Most of the time, his typical Chinese eyes were no more than thin slits that didn't allow one to even see his eyes. This time they were huge! With smoke and debris floating about, and his eyes so big, there must have been some sound coming from his mouth because it was wide open too—almost as if he were hollering which he probably was, but I don't remember any sound.

Maybe the noise of the blast had affected my hearing. The sound in his ears must have been something for him as well because his head was only two feet from the gun. There I am lying on my back on the ground, a gun across my chest, the back door of the car wide open, Tah Soak's face and eyes straining, the inside of the car filled with smoke, and a big gaping hole in the roof above the back door of this brand new car. I don't remember any other sounds other than that blast, but I am sure somebody must have done some screaming.

The first thing I did hear after the surprise blast and the total shock was my father hollering as he ran along the path from the greenhouses

towards us. Still on my back, I rolled my head to him. He was running and shouting.

In one of his hands he held a head of cabbage. I guess that was what we had come to get. In the other hand he clutched a knife that he had just used to cut the cabbage. The cabbage represented my head and the knife was how he was going to cut my head off with. No explanation needed here! I was out of there now! Up on my feet running full out in a fraction of a second. I didn't look back or hear anything. Why I ran the direction I did, I don't know. I guess it was perhaps because I was between the fence (thirty feet or so) and the side of the car. The fence was of barbed wire and separated our farm from the army reserve training fields. At full throttle I'm not about to pick my way through this obstacle especially with the mess that I had just created behind me. What consequences await me? I just dove as high as I could. A barb caught my pants as I came down and rolled in the dirt but that didn't matter. I was on my feet running flat out through the rows of vegetables of our market garden. The trees were about a quarter of a mile away, and I needed to get there to hide. By the time I did turn around to look I was crying a river and puffing hard. I saw Dad and Tah Soak looking over the damage of the car, but I just kept going. The bush I was in was no stranger to me because we spent a lot of time there. Dead trees often fell in the bush, and my brother and I would skid out the logs with the horses. We used the firewood in the greenhouse and for the hog cookers. Also we hunted for grouse and owls there. Sometimes our chickens would get loose from the pens and go lay eggs in that bush which we would try to find. Some of the very best berry picking was there, and we also played hide and seek there. None of that mattered now because, I just had to—to where I don't know—just get out of there!

I kept wandering and stumbling around. I was crying and worrying about what would happen to me. The last bit of bush was the raspberry patch near the north property line of the Chalmers' farm. After crawling through the thick raspberry brambles, I was scraped and scratched all over, but I was bound and determined to stay down and out of sight. I could see the neighbour's barn and thought that might be a place to hole up. If I stayed near the bushes besides the road, I could sneak to the barn without anyone seeing me. No one was around, so I climbed up into the hay loft and found a dark corner to lay down in. Still crying in spurts, I felt I'd better not make any noise or someone might hear me. I covered myself with straw and tried to be quiet.

When I woke up it was pitch black in the hay loft, and I was scared and cold. It didn't take long for the recent memories to come back of what I had done. My fright started all over again, and I began to cry. My eyes were filled with tears, and I was shivering in that dark place. I couldn't see a thing, and every time the animals down below made a sound I froze as if my time had come. I decided that, because I couldn't see in the darkness and I didn't know where to go, I might just as well stay there. Where would I go anyway? My family would all hate me for what I had done to their world with a new car. I dug myself deeper into the hay pile.

It was early morning when I carefully looked around and climbed down from the loft and headed for home. Every noise startled me as I slowly walked along the pathway on our farm that led to and from the Chalmer's place. The first glimpse into our farm yard revealed that no one was around. I tried to sneak past the turkey pen, and all of a sudden they began making a hell of a racket. Most of the time turkeys are noisy anyway, but at this particular time I felt as if they knew all about my plight and were mocking or laughing at me. I could have killed every one of them right about then. Once past the damn birds, things quieted down to my relief. I walked slowly down the road that crossed the field to the greenhouses. I checked carefully and found no one was there either. I picked some carrots and lettuce to eat, then into the greenhouse to down some tomatoes to relieve my hunger. I found an old sweater of Dad's and tried to cover up a bit from the chill. As I wandered through the plants, I tried to think of how I could run away, but where would I go? The world would hate me, my family would hate me, what could I do? Right about then I kind of hated me too.

I finally decided to face the music and take my lumps because I was wandering carefully across the open army training field towards home. I wasn't in any particular hurry because I knew there would be hell to pay. Rather than go through the army barracks or down the road which was a short cut to home, I picked my way through some bushes. When I got to the other side I could see our house. There was no car in the driveway, so that meant that Dad had already gone to open the café at about 6 am. At least Dad being gone was a relief!

When I walked in the back door and kitchen, there was Mom at the old kitchen stove. She whirled around to face me with knuckles on her hips and looked at me. *Oh boy*, I thought. *Here it comes.* I just stood there with my head held low. I was ready to run or duck or whatever, but it never came. Mom walked over and put both arms around me as I sobbed. She kissed me and softly talked to me and asked if I was all right. I was crying when she picked me up and carried me into her bedroom and tucked me into her bed. She said to be quiet, the other kids weren't up yet, and that maybe I should not go to school until tomorrow.

Anyone who has known about the Shotgun Sunroof over the many years of my life has never let me forget it. Although it is one of several awful embarrassing elements of my person, this one has hounded me through the years. However, my sad story has provided much hilarity and laughter for the many gatherings of my family and friends.

Not much was ever said to me by my father as I did my best to hide from him. He probably realized that he was as much to blame for the disaster as I was. He had left shells in the gun chamber. Tah Soak stayed pretty much to himself after that. He was probably deaf by then anyway. As for me, I was scarred both in body and pride that kept me in a low profile for some time. Dad never did take the car in to have the hole in the roof repaired. He just stuffed it full of paper napkins and hammered the flared metal back down into place as best he could. Maybe he did it as a reminder of what can happen with carelessness. It has been that for me! I never did get as friendly with that car as I had been before.

Unfortunately, I had lost my first love.

APPENDIX D

A Sister's Remembrance

by Nieta Wiedeman Duff

Betty was my oldest sister. She was the oldest of thirteen children, and I was the youngest, a generation apart.

I speak from hearsay because I was too young to remember when Betty was young or when she married Jack, but I have heard my siblings speak of the many things that Jack and Betty did for our family after our father died. They were instrumental in bringing the family to Grande Prairie where I grew up.

Betty was an important part of my life until I was eighteen. We lived in Grande Prairie, so I was always around the Marvins. We kids grew up together. Betty treated me like one of her own children, and long after I had grown up and left Grande Prairie, she treated me with continuing love just as she would her own children.

In those early years when our mother was still a young widow with young children to bring up, Betty was always there for Mom to talk to.

Memories of Christmas dinner at our house are vivid with Mom and Betty in the kitchen getting the turkey on the table for all of us, then a return visit to the Marvins' house for New Years for another turkey feast. When things were tough financially, Betty supplied an extra chicken or a dozen eggs from their farm, and at Christmas there was always a turkey.

Evelyn Marvin Millman

The day we left Grande Prairie to live in Edmonton, I can still recall vividly Jack and Betty standing in their yard with tears in their eyes as we drove away. I remember being deeply moved to think that I would be missed. It was the end of an era. Betty was no longer my Mom's emotional support.

Eventually, I left Edmonton and moved to Vancouver where I met my husband Bob. Betty was always positive about my marriage to Bob, and she was very fond of him. In fact, I have always believed that in a contest of popularity between the two of us, in Betty's eyes, Bob would have won. When our children came along, she loved them devotedly. She never forgot their birthdays and was always interested in what they were doing.

She had a great appreciation for the beauty of God's handiwork. She let us know how thrilled she was with the azaleas and rhododendrons which bloomed so profusely in our garden in Vancouver in the spring.

I suppose the main thing about Betty that will embody her spirit for me was her great zest for life. She didn't seem to get tired. I think a prime example of this was our daughter Kathryn's wedding three years ago. Betty could scarcely get around, but there was no way she was going to miss a party in Vancouver.

It was with great satisfaction that, when Kathryn and I visited her this last July as she was declining, she said to Kathryn, "I don't remember your name just now, but I was at your wedding."

These are a few of my memories of my sister Betty.

APPENDIX E

Bear Creek Flats

by Evelyn Millman

Bear Creek Flats in Grande Prairie was nothing special to me as a child. For my three siblings and I in the thirties and forties, it was just a long strip of low-lying hills and flat valleys along the Bear Creek on the eastern side of town. However, what was special there was my grandmother Wiedeman's home smack-dab in the middle of it. Her home was where we spent a great deal of our youthful days. It was where we settled for a few hours each week while we explored the nooks and crannies of the Flats. We thought of the Flats as where the poorer people lived because our grandma didn't have much money and her unpainted home looked drab.

Grandma's home was bounded on the back side by the Bear Creek, on the front side by a dirt road, and on the two other sides by vegetable gardens. Grandma moved there from the homestead fifty miles away during the Great Depression. Grandpa had died of a stroke, leaving her with thirteen children ranging in age from six months to twenty years. Grandma rented the only home available in Grande Prairie at a price she could barely afford. The small home was a simple shack, typical of many hastily built homes when the Peace River Country was just beginning to attract pioneers. Its floors, at first, were bare wood. Its furniture was homemade and crude. Beds were straw ticks with patchwork quilts made from old woolen coats. Dinnerware was tin. Sometimes water was rainwater from the roof. Sometimes it was melted snow in winter. Several years later a well was dug and a pump was installed in the kitchen. There was no such thing as indoor plumbing, telephone, electricity, television, radio or an indoor furnace. In today's terms, you can imagine what these hardships meant to a large family. But we were too young to notice. Almost everyone else we knew seemed to live the same way.

Mom would take us to visit Grandma and her clan about twice a week. We danced our way across the shaky wooden bridges spanning the gullies filled with poison ivy. As we peered down below, thoughts of the three Billy Goats Gruff ran through our imaginations. Running ahead of Mom, we finally got to the great hill directly in front of Grandma's gate and living room window. The hill was the largest one in the world. But gradually it got smaller as we grew bigger.

Sliding down that hill in winter was a challenge to see which one of us could manoeuvre our cardboard or sled through Grandma's gate. We hoped that Grandma was watching from her window, but we knew she was probably making noodles for our chicken soup or those wonderful fresh buns I can smell to this day. If it was Christmas day, she was tending the turkey and all the trimmings for her big family dinner. As we got older and more experienced on our sleds, we slid past Grandma's house right up to the town's main highway, stopping short of getting hit by the Model T Fords and the horse drawn drays.

Our Uncle Jake, crippled with polio at six months, climbed that hill with much difficulty every day to go to school. I think it kept him from dying too soon. My younger uncles dug a tiny cave in the side of the hill, which probably housed all the things that a secret hideout would contain for young guys. It was reinforced inside with timbers and padlocked on the outside. We wondered what was inside, as we sat on the hill nearby looking for wild onions. We might catch a glimpse now and then, but mostly it was off limits.

It was safe in those days for young children to go exploring on their own. I followed my aunt Nieta all over the meadows and valleys of Bear Creek Flats trying to find the first buttercups and crocuses in the spring. The trestle bridge that spanned the creek bed silently beckoned us to walk along its railroad tracks. We thought that if a train surprised us we would quickly get into the small overhanging shelters built onto the edges of the bridge in several spots. Despite our bravado we would have had all hell to pay if our parents had gotten wind of our shenanigans.

Bear Creek Flats was sparsely inhabited with a diverse mixture of European immigrants and aboriginals, The Toews family next to Grandma's house had a four-seat swing under their giant poplars that was very enticing in the hot summer. The residents of that home didn't seem to mind harbouring children in their yard, so we spent many hours on that swing. One day my big toe got caught between the boards of two opposing gliders. Ouch! I spent several days nursing that painful toe.

Despite the peaceful lifestyle of most residents, I remember some rather wild late night parties at the neighbours that scared the dickens out of me as I lay between Grandma and Nieta, on one of my sleep-ins. When Grandma got a knock on the door in the early morning hours, she would enquire in her broken German-English, "Wo ist dere?" through the door. She fearlessly fended off any unruly intruders with her no-nonsense manner.

Nowadays we seldom experience the tent caterpillar outbreaks that used to occur about every seven to ten years in Alberta. The Bear Creek Flats seemed more vulnerable to these scourges than the townsfolk up on the hill because it was warmer in the valley; however, everyone suffered for at least a month. It is hard to believe now that Grandma's house would be completely covered with tent caterpillars dropping from the giant poplars overhead. They seemed to be attracted to the unpainted exterior of her home, filling all of us with terror and dread that we might see one in our sheets or soup or shoe. We dared not step outside to slip and slide when squishing the caterpillars underfoot. We dared not venture on the gliding swing to have them fall into our hair.

Eventually Grandma moved away to the home of one of her daughters in the city to seek better circumstances for her remaining two children, Uncle Jake and Aunt Nieta. I think she was glad to leave the humble little house with its memories, both good and bad, and the Bear Creek Flats that had harbored her family for many years.

Today, after almost eighty years since Grandma rented her house, Bear Creek Flats is vastly changed. Except for a bit of caragana hedge and a lonely gatepost, all vestiges of my grandmother's home are gone. Although the great hill is still there, it is now landscaped with trees that make sledding impossible. The creek bed has been straightened and no longer meanders lazily through the Flats in graceful curves and falls. Most of the land has been bulldozed and levelled to accommodate more homes, a museum, parking lot, swimming pool and a senior's lodge.

If you enter the Bear Creek Flats through the western edge of Grande Prairie, you will notice one of the most beautiful city signs I have seen anywhere. On one of the few slopes still existing in the Flats, the sign in summer is surrounded with flowers welcoming you to the centre of a beautiful, thriving and friendly northern Alberta city that flourishes with the industries of agriculture, oil, gas and forestry and the attendant institutions of education, commerce, sports and the arts. Garlands of huge blooming flowers beautify the city centre lamp posts. Thanks to the abundant supply of late night summer sun, only in a northern city can one grow such grandiose blooms.

Progress has both its disadvantages as well as its advantages. Despite memories, time does not stand still. Vivid memories soon fade, undulating landscapes change, friends and families disperse. For now, our recollections will continue to evoke a time not so long ago, a time that, despite its hardships and privations, also had happy times, a time that produced men and women who have gone forth to build communities all over our nation so that the progeny of those days could enjoy what Grandma and all those of her generation dreamed for their children so many moons ago.

Evelyn Marvin Millman
March 24, 2013

260

MOON GATE

Evelyn Marvin Millman

CPSIA information can be obtained
at www.ICGtesting.com
Printed in the USA
LVOW06s1452110817
544632LV00010B/33/P